500 Reasons Why ...

I H
The
Office

Malcolm Burgess

Icon Books

Originally published in 2006
by Icon Books Ltd

This edition published in the UK in 2007
by Icon Books Ltd, The Old Dairy,
Brook Road, Thriplow,
Cambridge SG8 7RG
email: info@iconbooks.co.uk
www.iconbooks.co.uk

Sold in the UK, Europe, South Africa and Asia
by Faber & Faber Ltd, 3 Queen Square,
London WC1N 3AU
or their agents

Distributed in the UK, Europe, South Africa and Asia
by TBS Ltd, TBS Distribution Centre, Colchester Road
Frating Green, Colchester CO7 7DW

This edition published in Australia in 2007
by Allen & Unwin Pty Ltd,
PO Box 8500, 83 Alexander Street,
Crows Nest, NSW 2065

Distributed in Canada by
Penguin Books Canada,
90 Eglinton Avenue East, Suite 700,
Toronto, Ontario M4P 2YE

ISBN: 978-1840468-24-3

Typesetting by Hands Fotoset

Printed and bound in the UK by
Creative Print and Design Group

To my office … and Heather,
for everything

Contents

Malcolm Burgess is a journalist, scriptwriter and author. His comic series have appeared in *The Times*, the *Mail on Sunday*'s *You* magazine, the *Evening Standard*, the *Financial Times*, the *Guardian*, and *Metro*. He is also the author of *Forty-fied: How to be a Fortysomething* (Icon, 2007).

This book first appeared as 'The Office' series in London's *Metro*. 'The Corporate Bullshit Detector' (included in this book's final pages) first appeared in 'Creme' in *The Times*.

Introduction

Who, when they were six years old, ever said, 'Hey, I want to spend forty years of my life wondering what value-added knowledge capital is in a size-restricted cubicle surrounded by people who watch *Bargain Hunt*'? Apart from your boss of course.

If hell had a modern name, it would be today's workplace. Try as they might to convince us that there's a purpose to what we do (vision statements about global domination) and that they always have our best interests at heart (Human Resource managers who love us all), we know we're being conned.

And just because a few people – sorry, your boss again – are in the office every night, why should they make the rest of us feel like shirkers? It's not really surprising then that you may resort to minor acts of rebellion like slinking to the toilet in your coat and saying you may be some time (er, about fifteen hours).

Seriously, it's not you, it's them – your workaholic company or organisation and all its thousand and one indignities known to man and woman. You have to be pretty strange or overpaid or both – we promise not to mention your boss again – not to find it teeth-grindingly terrible.

Most of us dream of giving the ultimate leaving party speech, where we tell people what we really think about their stupid targets and sad behaviour (sorry, it's the last time we'll mention your boss). But it doesn't happen because either: (a) we aren't actually leaving; (b) we just break down speechless when handed the mini patio heater and card with all the signatures in suspiciously similar handwriting.

I Hate the Office is for everyone who's ever said: 'What the **** am I doing here?' With any luck it might even give you some extra material for your leaving party bile-a-thon.

Remember: today is the first day of the rest of your corporate life. Don't wait until the next Away Day in a budget hotel on a traffic island off the M25 where no one can hear you scream.

And you thought you were going to sit around laughing at actors in tights. Five reasons to hate ...

Arts-Based Training

Reason One: All right, your facilitator might not have thought four years' training to be the next Antony Sher would lead to this and a walk-on part in a Domestos advert. But then you didn't exactly expect to be standing on a chair in your socks in a Travelodge conference room, attempting to discover your Inner Corporate Clown.

Reason Two: It's soon clear that your facilitator: (a) can talk the back legs off a pantomime horse (he had enough experience at the Bedford Corn Exchange); (b) is obviously creative (he isn't wearing a tie); (c) wants to take you on a Life-Changing Journey.

Reason Three: Whether the course is 'Rediscovering the Internal Communication Vision' or 'Exploring Strategies for People and Organisations', you just know it will involve face-painting, feeling your partner's life force and taking off your shoes – so that you can't do a runner.

Reason Four: Not forgetting Blue Peter from Hell – with installations and human tableaux using bubble wrap, newspaper and lots of toilet rolls to explore Living With Corporate Uncertainty. Your facilitator stands triumphant amid a three-year-old's mess fest and people in strange Marquis de Sade positions.

Reason Five: Everyone knows that Shakespeare basically wrote his plays to deal with the urgent issues of call-centre communication and appraisal interviewing. That's why your group gets to role-play To Be Or Not To Be (Clarifying the Mission Statement), Hamlet and the Gravedigger (Dealing with Difficult People in a Customer Care Situation), and the Final Banquet Scene (Corporate Hospitality: The Way Ahead).

Just because you're out of the office, don't think they want you to enjoy yourself. Five reasons to hate …

Away Days

Reason One: Smart, smart casual, casual smart – whatever you decide to wear, it'll be wrong. Women are scared of anything that makes them look like Edwina Currie in civvies and keep to boring black; men usually end up in M&S chinos and look like they're attending a barbecue in Weybridge.

Reason Two: The venue must always look as if it's been rejected by the *Footballers' Wives* location manager for being too vulgar. If it's Spanish-Ranchero-Georgian with more than a touch of Ann Summers meets Lady Penelope's Creighton-Ward Mansion inside, you know you've got the right place.

Reason Three: Everyone talks about a never-very-special lunch as the high point of the day – like Bash Street Kids salivating at the sight of a sausage. This is because: (a) it's the high point of the day; (b) management might forget the embarrassing warm-up activity if you bond over the Beef Wellington.

Reason Four: It's brainstorm hell in there – as 35 people take six hours and 180 bottles of Badoit to decide the purpose of a meeting is to communicate. With ten minutes to go until the team 'trust' workshop, people like to stand apart – they feel they've bonded quite sufficiently – and wonder if being part of a human pyramid is really necessary.

Reason Five: By 4.30 pm you're plunged into depression, as you wonder: (a) who invented William Morris-scented bin liner gift packs and why am I buying them from reception; (b) are team leaders from Mars, Venus or somewhere outside the known Solar System; (c) what the hell am I doing here?

They have ways of making you hot,
sticky and very embarrassed.
Five reasons to hate …

Being Appraised

Reason One: Most appraisal claims make our CVs look as ethical as the Ten Commandments. Self-appraisal buzz-words include 'customer-focused' (knows when to avoid them whenever possible), 'teamworker' (enjoys letting other people do the work) and 'living the company philosophy' (carries a Next carrier bag like everyone else). Appraisal by your manager will actually require you to do some work – chiefly deciding how to take the credit for someone else's successful project.

Reason Two: Who needs office surveillance when you can have a 360-degree appraisal? Everyone must be able to comment on your performance and personality defects, from someone you once met in the corridor to the person who empties your bin.

Reason Three: In the public sector, it's all about 'competencies' – something has to justify your low salary. They're designed to make sure all public employees are singing from the same hymn sheet – just in case anyone shows a tendency towards creativity or dynamism and expects to be paid for it.

Reason Four: You must be seen to be continually expanding your job role, no matter how difficult this is. Even the Leafshine woman will need to suggest that she is constantly devising new strategies to make her Bizzie Lizzies grow smarter.

Reason Five: You're never honest about your manager's performance, stupid. Don't you just love it when they ask you for feedback at the end of the appraisal? Like you're really going to say they would benefit from instant trepanning or a seminar on 'How to Be a Human Being: A Guide for Beginners'.

When everyone's away, guess
who gets to do all their jobs?
Five reasons to hate …

Being Stuck in
the Office

Reason One: You know where you are in the office hierarchy by how much time you spend at your desk. One or two days a week makes you senior management – you must never do the coffee run/remember anyone's birthday/have a clue about office systems. Three to four days makes you middle management – ditto because you want to be senior management, except everyone's allowed to tut at you. Five days a week just means you're a very busy person indeed.

Reason Two: Congratulations – apart from your normal job description you've also acquired several hundred more, including: (a) answering everyone else's phone (at least there's a new person clients can blame); (b) manning the general enquiry desk for every passer-by (you obviously know everything and don't look at all busy); (c) sick report person (try not to gag at all those graphic descriptions).

Reason Three: Let's face it, angry couriers, unpleasant clients, lost strip-o-gram operatives, protesting cleaners, stroppy photocopier engineers and total strangers are all going to want to be your friend. Just what you always wanted.

Reason Four: In the absence of anyone important, Human Resources reluctantly has to let interviewees meet you. Hence the halting conversation at your desk – as you do your best to give an impression of efficiency and hope they don't notice the six-foot inflatable doll with dreadlocks under your desk (yes, you're the birthday party organiser as well: who else?).

Reason Five: Inevitably you start asking yourself philosophical questions. Why is stained beige the universal colour of choice for offices? Why does no one email on Friday afternoons? Why does my boss always think you need breasts to mail merge?

Do they want to be your friend – or is that a P45 you see before you? Five reasons to hate …

Being Taken Over

Reason One: Don't worry, just remember everything you did before was rubbish – even if nothing needs changing, they'll still want to do it completely differently. These changes will generally come under the headings of new: (a) work practices (they might actually expect you to have some); (b) visions (global empire to reach even more galaxies); (c) headcount (aka 'you're fired').

Reason Two: You're in duplicate – your spooky doppelganger roams a strange parallel universe with a job description and impossible targets just like you. But ask yourself can they dress up in a chicken suit and sing 'The Birdy Song' at the staff disco?

Reason Three: Even if they let you stay, you could face the trauma of an office relocation to somewhere up the M1, or an internal move to somewhere along a corridor previously felt to be too nasty even for temps and part-timers. It's not surprising everyone's suddenly busy with 'web-based research' – for the last few secure jobs left in the UK. Don't worry – the MD is doing it too.

Reason Four: There's bound to be another bald, middle-aged boss just like yours who thinks he can hold budget meetings at ten o'clock at night. In your worst nightmare scenario you find yourself working: (a) for neither of them – you're redundant; (b) one of them; (c) both of them. It's what they call a lose-lose situation.

Reason Five: From your duvet days (able to sleep at home as well as the office) and better maternity benefits (able to give birth out of the office) to gym membership (colleagues see you doing strange things with your body outside the office Christmas party) ... will they keep up your current range of incentives or suggest you're lucky to have a job? Have a guess.

Add up all the advantages of
working for your company.
This shouldn't take too long.
Five reasons to hate …

Benefits

Reason One: To counter our objections that we can't live on that kind of money, companies like to draw attention to their 'benefits' package – as if having simulated sex with a Swiss Ball in front of someone from Credit Control as part of our free gym membership is somehow preferable to a living wage.

Reason Two: Every time you commute, you think of your company and its interest-free season ticket loan. It doesn't just enable you to do a job you can't actually afford to do, but the thought of having to pay back the interest if you leave stops you looking elsewhere. Duh.

Reason Three: When they mentioned 'flexible working benefits' little did you realise it meant: (a) working between Christmas and the New Year because no one else wants to; (b) covering for any colleague whose tortoise is poorly; (c) not minding if your job is transferred at the slightest excuse to another part of the world very soon.

Reason Four: Private health plans let everyone know where they are in the office pecking order: the 'We Can't Afford to Have You Pegging Out On Us' package (for senior managers); the 'You're Safe Until You're Forty-Five' package (for middle managers); the 'You Can Always Ask the First Aider for an Aspirin' package (the rest of us).

Reason Five: We know they're trying for as many bullet points as possible, but including 'staff canteen' as a benefit is surely analogous to saying 'we value our employees and know how important subsidised Wagon Wheels are to their lifestyle'.

You always wanted to work
for a company with more
rubber plants than the rainforest.
Five reasons to hate …

Big
Organisations

Reason One: Their obsessive desire for you to bond with every other worker inevitably means sitting at an internal conference, between the woman who cleans the telephones and someone from facilities, and wondering how long you can seriously talk about smoked haddock?

Reason Two: They can't get enough of organisational 'change' – but fortunately experts say this takes up to ten years to happen. This reassures everyone that they won't have to know all the words of the new corporate anthem just yet.

Reason Three: Everyone says internal communications are a priority for big organisations, especially if departments are communicating by sending press releases to each other and a game of Chinese Whispers at the office Christmas Party would take about eleven years.

Reason Four: Staff only ever see the CEO on special streamed podcasts from his bunker when there's a major announcement of redundancies across five continents in the interests of, er, CEO salary increases. Or else at Christmas parties looking embarrassed because of the size of the latter.

Reason Five: Because they've never seen you before, staff from other departments regard you suspiciously and assume you must be: (a) an international terrorist; (b) the CEO; (c) the supplier who no one wanted to meet and who is still trying to find his way out two years later.

Go on then, break down,
they're all waiting.
Five reasons to hate …
Birthday Parties

Reason One: Sorry, they only appeal to people without children or too much time on their hands – not forgetting those who never had proper birthdays when young and now go into hysterics when they see a Mr Kipling cake. The rest of us just hide.

Reason Two: There's always one person who knows the Grotesque Card Shop backwards and likes to spend lunchtimes quality testing the latest bra-and-panties number for hilarity. And don't worry: they'll find a card to match your age perfectly. This basically means general cuddliness up to 21 (teddy bears and rabbits), after which decline sets in (gorillas' and elephants' backsides), leading to the terminal post-50s (otters wistfully going down holes).

Reason Three: The Birthday Watch Committee have ways of finding out your age. No amount of Botox or Pilates can keep this from them. They know you know the words to 'Lady In Red'.

Reason Four: Your exciting present (from Grotesque Card Shop) will be either: Life Begins at 40 liqueur glass in presentation box – complete with red silk rose for you to insert down your throat, or Muppet doll with sign saying 'Willing but not able'. It's probably the biggest surprise since Jade's IQ test results. Make sure you thank them from the bottom of your heart.

Reason Five: That's just the start. They won't want to forget all the badges, banners, party poppers and table decorations that every birthday person needs. Go on, give in: ask the MD to dance with you and your four-feet-high teddy bear.

Where would you be without them? Er, and vice-versa.
Five reasons to hate …

Bosses

Reason One: They're either micro-managers (know how many paper clips you get through in a day) or macro-managers (obsessed with company's '1000 Days to Total Global Penetration' plan). That's why they're bosses of course, and why you spend your days, er, counting paper clips or wondering if they're serious.

Reason Two: They need never do any work again thanks to empowerment (they feel sorry for you not being stretched enough), delegation (there's no one else they'd rather give their lousy jobs to) and facilitation (making it easy for all their work to go straight in your direction).

Reason Three: They like to impress us with every management theory going, but we still suffer from low productivity. At least they can blame you – you're obviously not working hard enough.

Reason Four: Having an MBA means they'll want to blue-sky everything and do role-plays in which you get to dress up and play the zeitgeist; a degree in Business Studies makes them prone to case studies and never doing anything original unless a focus group in Crawley agrees; while a 'Richard Littlejohn school of life' doctorate lets them go by their gut reactions but at least saves on flip chart paper.

Reason Five: Just because they don't look like *The Office*'s David Brent doesn't mean they don't have: (a) a hair-brained motivational scheme; (b) a grovelling relationship with senior management; (c) a trendy New Age phrase for 'work even harder'. They just won't be as funny unfortunately.

Your company's gone and got itself branded. We won't say as what. Five reasons to hate …

Branding

Reason One: If you're wearing a baseball cap with the company logo, reading an embarrassing script over the phone ('Hi, I'm John, I used to like metaphysical poetry at university.') or replacing the words of 'We Will Rock You' with your mission statement at the sales conference, you're 'living the brand'.

Reason Two: If people aren't multi-orgasmic at the mere sound of your company's name, expect branding consultants to intro-duce: (a) a new uniform to reflect your 'brand values' (blue nylon de rigueur); (b) transparency between employers and customers (you can see through the nylon); (c) positive customer experi-ences (not calling them 'yes' once in a while).

Reason Three: Consultants will encourage your company to promote a 'point of difference' from other similar products and make it a lifestyle choice. This may be fine for Apple but it's more difficult if you're dealing with extruded meat products from Eastern Europe that people would rather not hear about.

Reason Four: If all else fails, the only solution is for your company to 'reposition' and change its name – although it might be better if it's only a question of adding 'new', as in New Labour, otherwise an awful lot of neon T-shirts will be wasted.

Reason Five: We're all brands now – we're even supposed to see ourselves as 'own brand plc' with our own sales and marketing strategies. You know it worked well for the Beckhams – it's just a question of interesting *OK!* magazine in your Luxuri-ous and Fun-Filled Cubicle Week. Go for it.

You've got the posh corporate job
– now eat the cornflakes.
Five reasons to hate ....
Business Hotels

Reason One: Tripoli, Tashkent, traffic island off the M25 – they're all depressingly similar, wherever you are in the world. If you can't find a mini-bar with CCTV camera, air conditioning that never quite works, boring items of corporate art or a receptionist who can say 'trouser press' in 26 languages, then you should complain.

Reason Two: Everyone feels a need to behave corporately, and this usually means: (a) ordering the same breakfast as your senior manager opposite and trying to spell out the vision statement in All-Bran; (b) looking stressed to show you haven't checked your emails for at least two minutes; (c) visiting a colleague's room to make sure it's exactly like yours and they haven't got more mini body lotions than you.

Reason Three: You can always tell the class of business guests by their hotel meeting venues: the Bill Gates Suite suggests they own half the world's resources; an extension Portakabin means the public sector; while meeting in the reception area is usually reserved for desperate small-business people who give everyone their card – there's always a chance that someone will want a waistcoat knitted from dog hair.

Reason Four: Don't worry, the hotel gift shop has been specially screened to suit business customers. Gifts usually range from novels by John Grisham (you might have had a brain once) and Jeffery Archer (sorry, you never did) to shapeless cashmere sweaters (you have no taste but plenty of money) and model vintage cars (training courses do funny things to your mind).

Reason Five: It's assumed that Hugh Heffner, circa 1963, is your sexual role-model – you swinger, you. Hence *Emmanuelle 493*, *Sexy Secrets* and various euphemisms for Stuff Your Wife Finds Puerile and Sad on the hotel cable channel. Er, if you happen to be a woman, all we can say is that you shouldn't be.

You can't believe they're not nutters!
Five reasons to hate ...

Buzz Words

Reason One: With limited cubicle space and no natural daylight, and the person next door with more personal problems than the entire cast of *Hollyoaks*, it's not really surprising that most of us today are 'thinking outside the box' and seeking some 'windows of opportunity' too.

Reason Two: Members of your department go on an 'assertiveness training' course only so they can learn to say no to all the boring jobs and delegate them to someone else. No prizes for guessing who this person usually is.

Reason Three: Out go those long and boring job histories and lists of hobbies from our CVs. In come 'competencies' – like cross-channel implementation, best-practice delivery – i.e. those traits that would prove our capabilities if only we could work out what they actually mean.

Reason Four: We're going to scream if anyone boasts they're 'focused' because they're actually able to concentrate on one thing at a time. Ditto 'joined-up thinking' – if you can do joined-up writing there's no reason why you can't do the latter, so tell your manager to please stop showing off.

Reason Five: Outsiders have no idea what the 'ISO 9000 benchmarking system' is. Insiders aren't that clear either, as everyone becomes obsessed with Quality And Consistent Processes – it's Capital Letter Hell. Best to decide this isn't the 'glamorous opportunity with lots of fab showbiz types' they promised and engage in some Quality Job Hunting.

Please can we have your babies.
Five reasons to hate …

Client Entertainment

Reason One: It's sadly not enough for clients to simply offer you the contract in your office – they expect first to be properly entertained by seeing you: (a) choke on anything long, slimy or many-fronded; (b) ransack your collective unconscious for any micro-scrap of small talk lest they think you're desperate for their business; (c) ask the lap dancer for a receipt, please, for that twenty pounds.

Reason Two: You always seem to choose dishes that splash, squirt, drip, or require extensive finger-licking. But look on the bright side: that Jackson Pollock effect on your clothes at least gives you something interesting to talk about.

Reason Three: Choosing restaurants for foreign clients is a nightmare of strange cuisine (Latvian-Mongolian-Bolivian fusion), typical customer service (waiter won't talk to you as you're not Guy Ritchie), or having to explain what a jam roly poly is. You finally try somewhere they're bound to know. It's called McDonalds.

Reason Four: Talking shop straight away marks you as a corporate drone – but too much small talk about your daughter's guinea pig makes you feel guilty for choosing the most expensive items on the menu. You may just need to drink too much, and hope one of you remembers why you're there.

Reason Five: You're supposed to decide beforehand exactly why you're treating someone to a free lunch. Is this because it's depressing for: (a) the client to see the rest of your team; (b) you to see the rest of your team; (c) you to always eat chicken tikka sandwiches? If Accounts disputes the bill, tell them it includes a karaoke (i.e. you humiliating yourself and singing for your supper).

Tell them where to stick their
exclamation marks!
Five reasons to hate …
Coaches

Reason One: If coaching really works, why is the person your employer uses still hoping to move out of her garage? Whatever happened to their Ten Step Plan and the Unleashing of Their Personal Power? We honestly think they're keener to enter into a 'dependency situation' than we are.

Reason Two: We've all done the assertiveness training (twenty people in a meeting all saying, calmly and effectively, they won't do a thing) and the counselling (twenty people in a meeting asking for their needs to be met), and Inner Tennis (we always lose to Tim Henman). Now, thanks to our coach empowering us to become Ibiza Beach Away Day Consultants (our title of choice) there won't be anyone left to do the dreary tasks. Company-own goal again?

Reason Three: Apparently CEOs have been secretly coached for ages on how to get that Richard Branson man-of-the-people effect in their own working lives, and now feel it's time for others to find out how to wear a funny multi-coloured jumper without being mistaken for a breakfast-TV presenter.

Reason Four: Coaching also seems to be the new training because: (a) it's harder to fall asleep in a one-to-one situation; (b) there's a limit to how many 'Squeaking Professionally: Unlocking the Power of Your Voice' courses an individual can attend in one lifetime; (c) nothing else seems to have worked, does it?

Reason Five: Poor work/life balance? Stressed because everyone, like you, has chosen 123456 as a password? Worried that your Burberry Beanie Baby is so last year? No concern, it seems, is too great or small: your coach will help you find your Way Ahead. And, if all else fails, you too can become a life coach just like everyone else.

They love you all – that's why
they're leaving.
Five reasons to hate …

Colleagues Who
Are Leaving

Reason One: They are and you're not. Sorry, we think that's sufficient reason to hate them for their shocking disloyalty in going for another job that: (a) pays more; (b) has matching office furniture; (c) observes the EEC 48-hour work directive; (d) has a manager who says 'please' and 'that can wait until tomorrow'.

Reason Two: In the exit interview they can say all those explosive, jaw-dropping things you only dream about in your daily fantasy simulations. These include: 'my boss is a psychopath'; 'my colleagues are from planet Zog'; 'at least I've never said "let's fly it up the flagpole" at a meeting'. Cathartic.

Reason Three: Bright-eyed and bushy-tailed, they can come back and gloat. Given that their old job has probably gone, you could say: 'Management didn't think it was much of a role and the work experience boy didn't want it.' But you won't – as you're now doing it, on top of your existing job, for the same money. You could say 'sucker', but you won't.

Reason Four: Leaving parties are no surprise when everyone is leaving and pretending to break down at the thought of no more stationery requisition meetings. They're no surprise either because, such are the plethora of circulating envelopes, you've probably already contributed to your own future leaving present and six-feet-high padded card – though never more than ten pence, of course.

Reason Five: You'll seriously miss them, because who else will be the unofficial: (a) Office Kitchen Procurement Officer; (b) Birthday Events Manager; (c) Nurofen Supplier; (d) Toilet Roll Facilitator? Answer: you – don't get too excited.

Look, at least someone
wants to talk to you.
Five reasons to hate …

Communication

Reason One: Look forward to your colleagues' pathetic attempts at email communication: a few misspelt words without punctuation or grammar (MD); Bill Gates has spoken (IT department); Basil Fawlty has spoken (your manager). At least the office Popbitch editor (you) tries to be a little more amusing.

Reason Two: When all else fails, you know there are only two types of body language. When the boss is present, it's the 'I wish I had a pair of Gordon Gecko red braces' meets my 'I want to have the mission statement's babies' look. If he/she is absent, it's the 'I've got a pulse somewhere; please don't disturb me while I spend the next twelve months looking for it.'

Reason Three: Communication training courses usually involve an ex-RSC actor with twenty Magic Markers who offers senior managers ten surefire ways of telling the press: (a) nothing; (b) nothing very much; (c) unlike Enron, we give our employees bin bags to take away their misshapen cactuses.

Reason Four: Companies insist that communication is their first priority for staff and customers, which is why they like to send you on communication courses to discover your communication style (shouting now or saving it for later), develop active listening skills (stay conscious by listening for colleagues' sexual assignations during meetings), and do a customer roleplay (your chance to recreate the Mitchell brothers' fight from *EastEnders* and transfer it to a typical day in customer care shouldn't be difficult).

Reason Five: Like failed political parties, companies like to blame others for their lack of success in getting their message across, i.e. it wasn't their fault, honestly, it was the stupidity of their customers. This lets everyone off the hook and the communications team can claim another stunning victory.

It's the wrong type of rain again.
Five reasons to hate …
Commuting

Reason One: Why do you always sit next to the most boring person in the world and why are they always talking about: (a) what they'll be having for their tea; (b) the fact that it's raining while it's doing so; (c) how they've bought their Christmas presents eleven months in advance just to be on the safe side?

Reason Two: If you're a man it's essential that you read *The Da Vinci Code* and do your very best not to move your lips. If you're a woman, reading *Sharon Osbourne* is de rigueur as it at least lets you experience another dysfunctional family for a change. If you're an adult reading *Harry Potter* it's possibly a cry for help.

Reason Three: Newspapers, bags, coats, body fluids – we all like to put something between ourselves and others to give us an illusion of personal space. This includes those people who haven't been on a train since 1962 and think this gives them the right to berate others for their lack of sociability. Please, this isn't an episode of *Heartbeat*, sweetheart.

Reason Four: 'Adverse weather conditions' (normal British climate), 'staff shortages' (driver has trouble getting out of bed), 'late-running earlier train' (er, what?). No one believes these excuses anymore – certainly not your boss.

Reason Five: You consider all the alternatives from downshifting (eating lentils and making wind chimes) and working locally (exciting opportunities organising teenagers to dump free newspapers behind hedges and meet old school friends you've been avoiding for twenty years) to going freelance (euphemism for unemployment in the service industries). Exactly.

What do they mean, have
we switched it on?
Five reasons to hate …
Computers

Reason One: If we knew how to mend it, we'd do it, stupid. Most of us haven't a clue about PCs but faced with malfunctions, will press every control in sight. If nothing else, at least we discover the Ancient Greek alphabet and Regency ladies clip art. No wonder we like to decorate our PCs with postcards (we wish we were somewhere else), tinsel and fairy lights (we're pretending it's a Mexican peasant shrine in the absence of it being a working computer), or Post-its (we've got to pretend to do some work somehow).

Reason Two: Ever wondered where all your old Hobnobs, Cup-a-Soups, Pot Noodles and sandwich fillings get to? Answer: your keyboard is storing them up for a rainy day. If you're a temp, we hope you like somebody else's ten-week-old Mars Ice Cream in your fingernails.

Reason Three: If men are from Mars then Dave the IT man is from the Klingon homebase. His helpline gives a new meaning to non-customer service: you have very basic skills ('is it switched on?'), poor child control ('has your two-year-old been playing with your lap-top again?') or are a woman ('remove bracelets from moving parts'). Three days later he grudgingly visits your workstation.

Reason Four: It's confusing for Dave when suddenly everyone wants to be his girlfriend (or boyfriend) – especially when posh girls from Fulham ask about his favourite colour in their best blonde voices. But he doesn't have to suggest that you're either a person with very big fingers – or have recently had sex on your keyboard.

Reason Five: It's nice when things work again – er, we hadn't switched it on, actually – but we still want to smash Bill Gates's face in whenever that stupid smiley paperclip man pops up on our screens to show us how to write a letter and then freezes. Er, hello Dave, guess who?

They have ways of making
you hang on the phone.
Five reasons to hate …

Conference
Calls

Reason One: Everyone in the office is asked to be quiet because you have a Very Important Phone Call. Sadly, they know it really means your meeting was felt to be too unimportant for anyone to actually attend.

Reason Two: Of course you can't see your fellow participants – but you can hear their strange sounds. Welcome Sam the Sinus Woman, Derek the Trainee Dalek, Hannah the Heavy Breather, and Tom the Teeth Grinder. You either stop breathing so that everyone thinks you're dead, or attempt to engage in small talk: 'Er, did you have a long journey to the telephone?'

Reason Three: It might sound more exciting but, sorry, it's just another boring meeting. Except there'll be no opportunity for anyone to: (a) complain about the poor biscuit selection; (b) spill coffee down a neighbour's crotch, accidentally of course; (c) deal with your colleague's hair extension crisis.

Reason Four: There's no place for obvious body language like staring blankly or kicking someone under the table. Instead participants must resort to verbal signs which include 'mmmm' (look everyone, I'm thinking), 'yes' (I thought I ought to say something. Can I go home now?), and a bad coughing fit with death rattle (I'm choking on my blackcurrant tune. Save me.).

Reason Five: Everyone must sound unnaturally clear and stilted like a bad episode of *The Archers*. No one must interrupt anyone else lest they have to start their ten-minute monologue on payroll analysis again. The person with the most boring voice always gets their own way – agreed with a verbal sign from others. This is usually 'zzzzzzz'.

How do they know?
They don't even work here.
Five reasons to hate …
Consultants

Reason One: They earn a lot more than you and make recommendations that colleagues have been talking about for years in the office kitchen, but no one bothered to ask. Smarter and perkier than everyone else because they can afford Ozwald Boateng suits, aren't slumped at a PC for eight hours a day, and leave before their 'solutions' are put into practice.

Reason Two: They're often callow youths with recently acquired MBAs who will think nothing of informing workers with twice their age and experience that they need to be sacked in the interests of 'corporate synergy'.

Reason Three: Management consultancy trends come in fashions. In the 1980s, everyone was told to re-engineer, which led to 'outsourcing' and the employment of even more management consultants. The 1990s introduced the fashion for mergers and more sackings, but more caring this time as they provided Mansize Tissues. This decade is still waiting for the Next Big Management Thing. Suggestions on a postcard, please.

Reason Four: 'Growing Our Team: The Carriage Clock as Ultimate Incentive' ... 'Building Capacity: Using Spider Plants More Productively' ... 'The Peopleless Office: The Way Ahead, As If You Couldn't Guess'. Sorry, been there, done that, had the croissant.

Reason Five: They're prolific producers of scary consultation reports that no one understands, and for the workforce this is likely to mean the day of the dreaded black bin bags – usually stored in cupboards next to the last set of management consultancy reports.

You always wanted to meet
Carole Smiley, admit it.
Five reasons to hate …

Corporate
Hospitality

Reason One: It's an obvious oxymoron. Traditional packages from Wimbledon to Ascot include champagne cocktails in the Winners Club (air-conditioned shed), fast-track entry (you bet, at that price), and being mistaken for a minor Royal (not difficult). If clients don't award your company more orders, you'll let everyone know they're only C2s and wanted prawn cocktails.

Reason Two: If you wondered what happens to annoying sitcom stars or makeover show presenters between TV series – they're being overpaid this time to keep corporate clients awake. Wouldn't you want Lowri Turner to be associated with your new toilet plunger?

Reason Three: Such is the boredom of preceding events that everyone looks forward like small children to receiving a humiliating 'goody' bag at the end – think magazine-cover-mounted gifts you always throw away, corporate brochures and a Ferrero Rocher chocolate. Usually handed out by graduate PRs who studied Dostoyevsky at university.

Reason Four: The MC is frequently a local radio presenter who makes Alan Partridge look like Alain de Botton. Keeps the audience just this side of somnolent by making phallic suggestions with microphone/making them sing 'Tie A Yellow Ribbon'/threatening to sit on their laps.

Reason Five: Alarm bells should ring if clients are invited to your office after work for a cost-saving Giant Scalextric Around the Cubicles or It's a Knockout in the Atrium. You don't mind serving drinks but, sorry, you draw the line at pretending to be a 1961 Ferrari 156 or climbing through hoops as a seven-foot furry budgie.

We've given you a free profiterole –
now please like our product.
Five reasons to hate …

Corporate Launches

Reason One: We all know how awful and embarrassing they are, but just how terrible depends on: a) using a corporate events company that tries to recreate Pink Floyd's 'Live at Pompeii' gig in a Thurrock hotel; b) having a small budget and using 'this is the end of my career as I know it' staff dressed as walking, talking Jaffa Cakes; c) the time of year – it's never too cold to see women dressed in 'ironic' Austin Powers-style glamour.

Reason Two: Everyone tries not to smirk when the Chief Executive sees a new mouse mat as the Eighth Wonder of the Word – or a D-list celebrity does the same and everyone wonders whose product life will be reaching its sell-by date first.

Reason Three: The guest list acceptances are avidly perused by excitable corporate PRs in the naive belief that BBC news would seriously wish to report on the launch of plywood computer furniture promoted by an ex-star of *Howard's Way*. Leave that to the local media.

Reason Four: Let's be frank: free plonk and nibbles are the only reasons most people attend these functions in the first place – ranging from breakfast for journos who sadly don't have a life, to GI Diet raw meat skewers for finicky fashionistas.

Reason Five: Probably the only thing that gets us through it is looking forward to the free T-shirt at the end reading: 'I sold my soul to the corporate machine and all I got was this lousy T-shirt.' Go on, hate yourself.

If you think your job is bad –
you may be perfectly right.
Five reasons to hate …

Crap Jobs

Reason One: If you're stuck in a cubicle doing something that vaguely contributes to global capitalism though you're not quite sure what and you find yourself day-dreaming about: (a) masturbating pigs; (b) feeding George Galloway Whiskas; (c) meeting Jodie Marsh, then you've probably got a crap job.

Reason Two: 'Person Friday urgently required!' (all the boring jobs and a stupid name to go with it) … 'Earn £££££!' (Selling Double Glazing) … 'Applicant must possess initiative!' (able to successfully operate photocopier). You know you've got a seriously crap job if even the recruitment copywriters can't lie about it. (Note: exclamation marks don't make crap jobs sound like fun – they just identify them as crap jobs.)

Reason Three: Most of us have a good idea what the crap jobs in our company are. They're the ones our boss doesn't want to do but doesn't mind us doing while he adds them to his job description.

Reason Four: If you're under 25 you're automatically expected to be in a crap job, because it didn't do your boss any harm working ridiculous hours for not much money. If you're lucky you might get promoted to a slightly less crap job – let's face it, anything else you do in the company will appear impossibly glamorous even if it's just an eighth share in a hot desk.

Reason Five: Seriously crap jobs that nobody wants have to be 'outsourced' to agencies who'll find overqualified staff like ex-Professors of Physics from Albania, who see them as a way of one day working in a cubicle – just like yours …

Lovely doodles, darling, but
don't give up the day job.
Five reasons to hate …
Creativity

Reason One: Once limited to strange artistic people and the person who decorates the Secret Santa box, for anyone to now admit they're not creative is like saying 'I haven't had sex since 1978'. Conventional management solutions having failed, the hope now is that by making us crawl around on the floor in Unleash Your Inner-Corporate Creative Tiger courses we'll see a way ahead – it's probably called the exit.

Reason Two: It may be worth considering why, if creativity's so wonderful, out-of-work actors are so desperate to work in corporate environments and run dance drama role-plays of Edward de Bono's Six Thinking Hats. We think we should be told.

Reason Three: No one is still quite sure what being 'creative' in the workplace really means and whether you can actually be too 'creative', e.g. doing a Role Reversal and having your line manager perform all your tasks and then sob uncontrollably to be taken back to his BlackBerry.

Reason Four: According to a fashionable new theory, the creative classes like to congregate wherever there's a coffee shop with a wi-fi and a recent sighting of Chris Morris. However, we're still not sure if having done a 'Beginner's Guide to Brain-storming' course entitles us to hang out with Sadie Frost just yet.

Reason Five: Managers are forced to bring in 'creatives' under cover of darkness because it suggests the 'Mind Mapping for Right Hemisphere Thinking' Away Day has only taught people how to make better shopping lists.

No one knows the number of
posteriors they've seen.
Five reasons to hate …

Creeps, Office

Reason One: Up-managing? Isn't that just a poncy word for craven grovelling for promotion that makes Alan Partridge's lapdancing seem understated? But we accept there are degrees of grotesque behaviour – from slight Uriah Heep ('that's a very interesting target you have there') to Smithers from *The Simpsons* ('let me help facilitate your target') to Complete Slimeball ('I want to have your target's quadruplets').

Reason Two: Those office guru books just seem designed to make office brown-nosers of us all. Isn't turning yourself into 'brand me plc' just another term for advanced megalomania? Who wants to pack their briefcase a week in advance and worry that a carrier bag is career death? The pursuit of excellence went that-a-way.

Reason Three: We all know about fast-trackers with their nice suits and copies of *Management Today*, and how they actually enjoy working in your office. Of course they do – unlike you, they're only there temporarily. Think of your team as a mere pod designed to help these corporate cuckoos take over the world.

Reason Four: More and more companies are asking to see 'evidence-based' documentation to prove that you don't spend days searching the web for your next holiday. If your creepiest colleague isn't keeping their learning-skills log up to date, it's only because they're much too busy.

Reason Five: Volunteering to write music for the mission statement, working ridiculously long hours, telling the senior manager how great they looked in their polar bear Y-fronts at the office Christmas party ... If that's the only way to get a promotion, most of us will prefer to carry on sleeping with our team, er, in meetings.

Legal, truthful and honest?
Of course you are.
Five reasons to hate …
CVs

Reason One: Lies, lies and more lies – obviously the greatest work of fiction since *War and Peace*. But is it a mystery (determined not to give your age or reasons why you were repeatedly sacked), romance (mainly with yourself it would appear), epic saga (lists every training course you've ever been on), or a thriller (reader wants to solve enigma of how you've successfully evaded seventeen HR departments and where it will all end)?

Reason Two: If all else fails you can always try harder with your 'personal interests': 'enjoys sport' (stays awake for World Snooker Championship); 'enjoys travel' (goes on holiday); 'enjoys current affairs' (reads free newspaper); 'enjoys decorative arts' (does own wall papering).

Reason Three: We all know that we're too young and inexperienced, too old and expensive or, for a couple of years, the right age but the wrong sex in too many job applications. We sometimes wonder why we bother.

Reason Four: Everyone's CV should include an attention-grabbing personal profile (basically 40 words on why the company mission statement is really all about you), together with your achievements (how you added value to your previous job by deciding to work on Fridays occasionally), while ensuring there are no inconsistencies (checking you have only one name).

Reason Five: All those evenings you've spent 'working on our CV' and now they're saying they don't accept CVs. You only hope there's a place on their stupid form to mention everything that makes recruiters pay attention including your: (a) gerbil's name; (b) favourite colour; (c) partner's hobbies; (d) personal interpretation of *The Da Vinci Code*.

Always remember they're
nothing to do with you.
Five reasons to hate …

Customers

Reason One: Everything's so customer-focused these days it's not surprising we like to keep them at bay for as long as possible with a: (a) website containing inaccurate information and no phone number; (b) switchboard system that goes round in circles; (c) helpline in an indeterminate country which claims never to have heard of the product.

Reason Two: Because they can't find any real customers, many companies now claim to have 'internal customers'. No one quite understands why, but at least it gives everyone something to do, although with fewer opportunities for the sales team to collect soaps-on-a-rope from budget business hotels.

Reason Three: Companies like to offer you role-play training in becoming 'customer-friendly' – in case you ever wanted to know what it was like doing a bad Victor Meldrew impersonation in front of total strangers in a Kirkcaldy motel.

Reason Four: Should you ever grotesquely have to come into contact with real-life members of the public, let them know in advance that this is only your temporary career – while you decide whether to continue with the advanced brain surgery.

Reason Five: Should any customers slip through, you may need to use 'customer relationship management'. This is just a matter of sending them a set of miniature golf clubs that can be used as cocktail sticks to advertise your brand values. This should keep them gobsmacked for a while.

Too young, too old –
why do we bother?
Five reasons to hate …

Discrimination, Age

Reason One: If under 25, you must be: (a) 'enthusiastic with a great sense of humour' (you'll need it when you find out you're paid half of what everybody else gets); (b) grateful to get the jobs even the temp refuses; (c) constantly reminded of the University of Life by jobsworths whose idea of risk-taking is to borrow someone's stapler without asking.

Reason Two: If you're between 25 and 40 you're bound to be: (a) keen to see work as the New Sex, so limited is your time with your partner; (b) involved in a more intimate relationship with an M&S chill cabinet than with the latter; (c) feeling guilty about taking your holiday entitlement with your 'secret' family.

Reason Three: If you're over 40, you must be: (a) incapable of learning anything new and technological – you still get excited when you receive an email; (b) expendable – you won't mind being made redundant at the first sign of a recession; (c) so resentful of anyone younger you keep a pyre for burning Top Shop ads.

Reason Four: If you're over 60, you must be: (a) the only person left who knows where the plastic Christmas tree is kept – they have to keep you on; (b) the only person who knows about the MD and the photocopying incident at the office Christmas party last year – ditto; (c) receiving an awful pension.

Reason Five: If you're over 70 in an office you must be lying about your age. But look on the bright side – at least you'll be missing *Doctors* and *Countdown*.

We've got to get out of this place – but where to? Five reasons to hate …

Daydreams

Reason One: You blame it on all those exercises asking us where we want to be in five years' time. Since they asked, your down-shifting destiny lies in a Welsh commune with disillusioned *Guardian* readers/finally learning to make felt handbags and selling the results to people in Primrose Hill. Feel the fear but remember how much of nature Hugh Fearnley-Whittingstall slaughters on a daily basis.

Reason Two: With your extensive range of different writing styles from stream of consciousness (your latest report) to children's (writing clear instructions for your MD), you seem to think you could be a famous author. Except it usually takes loads of talent. Best to work on your CV and hone your fantasy style.

Reason Three: Of course there's always working from home: no more endless meetings, office politics or commuting. Until you realise your only meaningful social interaction for the next 25 years is likely to be with cats, Avon ladies and Jehovah's Witnesses.

Reason Four: You're seriously thinking about emigrating to France, South Africa or Australia. Looks like someone's been watching too many 'I Wish I Could Be Anywhere But Here' TV programmes and hasn't see the one about cleaning ex-pats' pools.

Reason Five: Sorry, sunlighting's just a poncy new word for doing two backbreaking jobs – and having two nervous break-downs – instead of one.

Beige, beige, beige – and
preferably sticky.
Five reasons to hate …
Design, Office

Reason One: Er, flickering neon lights, faded beige PCs, yucky keyboards, festering kitchens, recycled air that's been in circulation since 1977. No wonder they expect you to be very focused (hopefully, you won't have any time to notice).

Reason Two: Receptions are meant to be the window of the corporate world, which is why they range from minimalist (shame about the non-matching staff) and Argos catalogue (1994 edition) to eighties chrome and black (management still in denial about Mrs Thatcher's resignation).

Reason Three: Executive offices must have doors so that they can be closed by your boss all the time (crisis management), most of the time (worried that his 118 Blue-Skying Magic Markers might be stolen), or only sometimes (open door policy – needs to find out latest football scores).

Reason Four: Every office must have a permanent photocopier queue because someone is always photocopying 'The Dooms-day Report' and breaking the machine, while everyone waits for an engineer to tell them it's broken and to blame it on their illegal sexual activities.

Reason Five: Most office designs make even our front rooms seem like a vision of Stalinist planning. It's unergonomic hell in there, as they pile in new cubicles and work stations – at least battery hens get to make a quicker exit. But remember your job description asks you to be 'flexible' (so try not to mind being separated from Tracey's 24/7 'how I stop my finger-nails from breaking' monologue by one millimetre of chipboard).

If you're not wearing the right shade of black, they'll want to know why. Five reasons to hate …

Dress Codes

Reason One: Everyone tells you to 'dress for the job you want, not the job you have' but since this consists of lying on a chaise longue inside your luxury apartment dictating your bestseller, or just sitting at home in your pyjamas, you don't find this very helpful.

Reason Two: Others tell you to dress like your boss and to even match her briefcase and umbrella if you want promotion. You're already supposed to be copying her body language and management catchphrases – couldn't she make it easier and just go for genetically engineered Viyella team cloning instead?

Reason Three: You tried hard with Dress Down Days, honestly, but know you looked hideous as no one knew what 'smart casual' meant (certainly not the people in HR: were they born in black business suits?). It might have been easier just to come in naked – that way we could have got our varying degrees of unsuitable body exposure out of the way and settled down to discuss *Desperate Housewives*.

Reason Four: Why don't they just tell you to wear boring clothes unless you're an advertising creative or a failed dotcommer – in which case you're allowed to wear jeans and to pretend to be Mick Hucknell, circa 1989.

Reason Five: Choose your item of presenteeism clothing with care. After all, when you finally tell them what you think and do your Lord Lucan disappearance act, do you really wish a shapeless acrylic woolly stuffed with tissues to be your lasting memorial? Don't let the bastards …

Look, we don't care if it's real or artificial, go away.
Five reasons to hate …

Early Signs of Xmas

Reason One: An email has already gone round suggesting Christmas lunch options: Traditional English (hand-slaughtered by Bernard Matthews), Foreign But Not Trying Too Hard (The Night Before Christmas Curry), Foreign Pretentious (over-eating sounds better in French) and 'We're a Christmas-Free Zone' (chips and nasty yoghurts as usual).

Reason Two: The Don't They Know It's The Office Christmas Party Committee narrows down the theme to a 'Past Times Victorian Christmas'. Sadly, budgets don't stretch this far – people are reminded that the purple tinsel and Slade tape are still in the cupboard.

Reason Three: A young and enthusiastic committee member suggests a Christmas post-box for colleagues' gifts and cards. Everyone is too embarrassed to say no and an outsize toilet roll is covered in red crêpe paper and cotton wool balls, with a perky robin on top.

Reason Four: Excuses for not attending the office party start flooding in. They range from 'I'm out of the country all of a sudden' and 'I've got an urgent dental appointment' to 'I've got an allergy to Kettle Chips'.

Reason Five: General Christmas, angst-filled conversations include: 'What's this year's Christmas colour and will it matter anyway as most people under strobe lights look as if they've got psychedelic chicken-pox' and 'what colour matches vomit down you after a full turkey course?'

They can't wait to get out of here fast enough. Now why would that be?
Five reasons to hate ...

Fast-Trackers

Reason One: They haven't operated a photocopier since 1999, won't stay in a job more than two years, and have had more exit strategies than you've had, er, piles of photocopying. If yours isn't CEO of one of the anti-globalisers' most hated corporations by the age of 35, everyone will want to know why.

Reason Two: They walk the horrible talk. Their job title usually includes 'Strategic' and 'Quality' and makes everyone else feel like pig slops. If you can explain your job to a six-year-old in under five seconds then, sorry, you're definitely not in the fast-track league.

Reason Three: They always have game plans, which usually involve extensive networking (going out to lunch with someone whose job they want), mentoring (ditto, and also stealing their best ideas), and attending conferences (not eating all the sweeties or falling asleep while someone reads from their Power-Point presentation).

Reason Four: They hate eBay's founder Jeff Skoll for being the fast-trackers' fast-tracker and getting there before them. They just hope no one remembers their own dot.com over-excitement and short-lived belief that cargo trousers made them look tragically hip and not just four-feet tall.

Reason Five: They have a Life Coach to learn about Prioritising Needs (theirs of course), Developing Listening Skills (in case anyone's talking about them), and Speed Networking (use it as speed dating – they don't have time for sex otherwise).

We know this isn't in your job
description, but ....
Five reasons to hate ...

Female
Stereotypes

Reason One: If you wear a skirt and have successfully resisted job mobility for more than six months then you'll be honorary resident shaman and automatically know: (a) where the spare toilet rolls are kept; (b) where the Christmas decorations are kept; (c) the telephone number of everyone in the company. Basically anything boring that nobody else can be bothered to remember.

Reason Two: If you're a woman they like to volunteer you for extra responsibilities as Fire Officer, First Aider and as Departmental Rep on the Health and Safety Committee discussing sensible kettle management. Enjoy.

Reason Three: Shopping is always something close to a woman's heart, isn't it? Which is why you're only too happy to add personal shopper to your lengthy job description. Forgotten presents for your boss's wife are your forte, while purchasing another woman's tights gives you a great deal of pleasure.

Reason Four: Having done a half-day 'First Aider's' course (mainly involves French-kissing an inflatable doll which resembles Princess Anne) everyone will assume you have universal medical knowledge. They'll ask advice about their gynaecological problems and will want to let their severed fingers bleed all over you. All you can do is faint and explain you're not allowed to give them paracetemol.

Reason Five: Only basic listening skills and access to a public thoroughfare are needed before any woman can graduate to departmental agony aunt and run her own unofficial drop-in centre. Is it because you don't really matter? How many psychodramas can one team have? Tell us the truth – or on second thoughts, don't.

Sorry, they can't be serious,
it's raining out there.
Five reasons to hate ...

Fire Drills

Reason One: If the MD's PA is leaving her Manolos behind, you know it's definitely not the real thing. But if you haven't got a coat or umbrella, you know it's definitely going to be the wettest day of the year.

Reason Two: Your Fire Marshal will be someone who: (a) wanted to be in *London's Burning*; (b) enjoys using a loudhailer in restricted spaces; (c) doesn't normally get much attention – keeping a fire extinguisher and axe under their desk and a fluorescent tabard on their chair should do something about this.

Reason Three: Inevitably, we all go back for personal belongings, reflecting our arrested personal development. These range from your matching set of office Trolls ('they're all that lie between me and the void') to your clean mug ('someone else will use it') and files ('I'd rather burn alive than lose my performance indicators').

Reason Four: People are divided between those who take it seriously and those who see it as an opportunity to explore other departments and see who's got a bigger litter bin than them.

Reason Five: Grouping outside, you're with lots of blinking co-workers you've never met before, some of whom may not have seen daylight since the mid-eighties. It's like the office Christmas party but without the Twiglets. Though at least you're missing work, so it can't be all bad.

Always remember, first
depressions count.
Five reasons to hate …

First Day, The

Reason One: You always arrive much too early and soon worry whether you can: (a) maintain that strange 'I want your job' look that so impressed the interviewer; (b) remember all the lies and half-truths in your CV; (c) spot the person you'll be next to – Angry Person, Diva, or Pre-infantile And Obsessed With Fun-Fur Anthropomorphic Objects.

Reason Two: You now question whether wearing your smart interview outfit again was such a good idea: colleagues wonder if a Mormon missionary has got into the building by mistake.

Reason Three: It won't take you long to discover why your pre-decessor moved on to 'further exciting opportunities elsewhere'. But at least the five years' worth of mismanagement and filing they left behind will keep you occupied for some time.

Reason Four: Colleagues try to foist on you all the boring depart-mental roles no one else wants, from Stationery Requisition Officer (death by collapsing ring binders) and Kitchen Monitor (death by bacteria) to Investors In People Rep (death by tick list).

Reason Five: You do the induction course and receive the shiny handbook but wonder why none of it bears the slightest resem-blance to what's going on around you. You keep your head down and breathe a sigh of relief; admit it, you were worried for a moment.

Er, at least the MD's wife
said she liked it.
Five reasons to hate ...

Focus Groups

Reason One: The people at head office, who don't really get out very much, suddenly realise it's not enough just to ask token staff stereotypical questions about new product ideas (e.g. under-25s are supposed to know about the Arctic Monkeys; ditto over-50s and stair-lifts). Instead, they must ask target audiences in focus groups similarly stereotypical questions. This will only confirm what the office cleaner said about the idea of a sausage-flavoured milkshake, but will cost a lot more.

Reason Two: Focus-group members usually sit in a strange recreation of a set for 1980s breakfast TV while the 'facilitator' asks: (a) which celebrity they identify the product with; (b) which car might a sausage-flavoured milkshake drive; (c) what is the product's view on Tom and Katie?

Reason Three: All creative staff are kept well away lest it prove too depressing when group members reveal that they associate their new product with Michael Barrymore and the Liberal Democrats.

Reason Four: Focus groups consist mainly of Weird People Who Don't Seem To Be Working But Think They Know Everything About Products No One Really Wants. They're famous for such popular concepts as I Can't Believe It's Not Butter!, New Labour and most Hollywood films since 1980. Enough said.

Reason Five: They also consist of People Who Are Working But Don't Mind Wasting A Day when used by HR departments for 'internal communications' purposes. With any luck, they'll come up with some nice new names for downsizing, restructuring and redundancies. Keep it feel-good, please.

Is it really worth bothering?
Five reasons to hate …

Going Away

Reason One: Holidays are the new work. To cope with your time away, expect to spend long hours instructing your mini-mes with the most thought-out action plan since the Battle of the Bulge. Don't even think about what happens when you get back. Feel very guilty, by the way, for actually taking your holiday entitlement. Who do you think you are – Tara Palmer-Tompkinson?

Reason Two: Holidays are the failed work/life balance. With pre-holiday work so manic, it's not surprising that you cancel your cat, milk and children and end up packing your office clothes. You know it doesn't make sense.

Reason Three: Holidays are the new anxiety inducers. Forget: 'Did I leave the fridge door open?' Now look forward to having panic attacks about: (a) office politics; (b) coming back to all the post no one else wants; (c) losing your job. Along with the Christmas break and parents' funerals, it's the time of choice for companies to 'let people go'. Don't bother asking how they'll cope without you – they will.

Reason Four: Holidays are the new snobbery. It's not enough that you're going on holiday: are you going on the right holiday? Anywhere that doesn't require you to wear thrombosis socks on the journey is so Tracey and Darren from Accounts. Ideally, your holiday should include a dangerous, near-death experience in the developing world, but preferably with room service.

Reason Five: Summer holidays are the new post-coital depression. It's funny how they throw everything into perspective – your long hours, your boring colleagues, your spider plant. Don't worry. Only 50 weeks until your next one.

You know it's always embarrassing for them to talk about money.
Five reasons to hate …

Having to Ask for a Rise

Reason One: Only you and your mum know what a dynamic key player you are. Everyone else (including your boss) knows that you: (a) had auto-erotic sex with a bin liner at the office Christmas party; (b) last spoke in a meeting in 2001 to ask where the Mint Imperials were; (c) can't find enough time to deal with all your personal emails during the day. You may need to bow to the inevitable and cry now.

Reason Two: To get what you want you're supposed to copy your boss's body language. In his case this normally means falling asleep with extra dribble, rearranging yourself very publicly, or sighing adenoidally.

Reason Three: Don't worry, no matter how carefully your strategy is worked out, you always end up with a nervous rash that makes you look like Spider Man having a hot flush.

Reason Four: Bosses like to protect themselves by claiming it's either the wrong time of the year (er, any month with month in it), or that profits are down (there's only enough for their pay rise). They may like to make you feel better by reminding you about your already very generous benefit package (luncheon vouchers based on the 1983 Cost of Living Index).

Reason Five: Bosses are congenitally programmed to say 'no' at all times, so the experts tell us to have some options from Terribly Embarrassing ('When I think what I did for our Through-put Situation brainstorm ...') to Personally Humiliating ('I'm having to take office toilet paper home ...').

Go on, welcome them to the
real world.
Five reasons to hate ...

Head Office

Reason One: Even if the work can be done just as well by people in their slippers in back bedrooms, companies still like to have a post-modern headquarters that includes: (a) an atrium with wall-to-wall Amazonian rain forest where the Leafshine woman was last seen alive in 2001; (b) mission statement posters claiming it's the 'Number One Global Leader' and totally caring – except a bit more obfuscatory in case anyone actually reads it and wants to get awkward.

Reason Two: It's very much 'them' and 'us' – 'they' provide you with all the leadership and business plans and a dodgy contacts list, to try and sell a product acclaimed by a focus group of students bribed with a slice of free pizza.

Reason Three: Whether your head office is in London, New York or Sydney, they'll want to tell you things like they're at the interface of global value propositions analysis. Very little of this will be in English as you know it and it may need translating to let you know what it really means.

Reason Four: In order to break down those difficult barriers between HQ and the rest of you, they like to provide: (a) a special newsletter (death by exclamation mark!); (b) motivational days (the woman who transformed M&S and removed all the kilts helps you get in touch with your 'inner brand'); (c) a 'buddy' system (someone called Tarquin wants to be your friend).

Reason Five: Head office likes to meet staff it's managing virtually at least once a year so that it can put a face to a redundancy. After all, someone's got to pay for HQ staff's personal massage consultants.

They know who you are,
don't you worry.
Five reasons to hate …

Human Resources

Reason One: Time past when they were called Personnel, their job was to wear fluffy jumpers, show an abnormal interest in your hobbies at your interview and, if you were successful, show you where the toilet was. Today they see themselves as much more important and aggressive: you're basically ballast and may be surplus to requirements at any moment.

Reason Two: Remember, thanks to psychometric testing, 360-degree appraisal and surveillance, they know everything there is to know about you, including your unfortunate impersonation of your line manager at the sales conference semi-naked and in extension hair pieces, unless you can prove it was just an unsuccessful Victoria Beckham impersonation.

Reason Three: Don't ever think you can get one over them in an interview by having a foolproof CV or getting all the questions right, as the person from HR knows that the Chief Executive actually had an idea recently and wouldn't want to hear about any from you, especially if they make sense.

Reason Four: Essential skills for today's HR professional include: (a) change management – explaining your exciting job option, i.e. redundancy; (b) implementing lifelong learning – another training course where staff have to tell colleagues they've sat next to for six years their names; (c) corporate branding – telling you to take down your posters in the interests of the corporate beige walls statement.

Reason Five: In the event of your line manager agreeing to a change in your working conditions, it will always be subject to HR agreeing that giving you access to a non-wobbly chair for a trial period won't create an unfortunate precedent among other staff.

Sorry, we are not amused.
Five reasons to hate …

Humour, Office

Reason One: Colleagues emailing you pictures of nude male Australian free-fall parachutists is equivalent to your next-door neighbour popping pornography through your letter-box on a regular basis because they 'thought you might like to see it'. A spectacular close-up of course usually freezes just as your manager arrives at your desk.

Reason Two: Office posters that say 'You don't have to be mad to work here but it helps' or 'You want it when?' and those life-size Wombles, Zippy from Rainbow or Steve Zodiac from Fireball XL5. Are the latter supposed to be funny, as in retro, post-modern funny – i.e. 'I'm a sad 32-year-old obsessed with my TV-infatuated childhood' – or just extremely sad?

Reason Three: More and more firms feel the need to bring in their touchy-feely laughter specialists (est. 1998 and laughing all the way to the bank) for workplace training. Get ready for 'Seeing the funny side of downsizing' and 'A funny thing happened to me on the way to the ISO 9000 meeting'. Try not to get too hysterical.

Reason Four: Many companies ask for people with 'a sense of humour' in their recruitment adverts: this is mainly for when you see your final salary. But jokes in an interview are likely to backfire as there is sadly a good chance someone present is: (a) a woman; (b) racially tolerant; (c) non-homophobic; (d) has relatives in Essex.

Reason Five: Leaving parties involving Tarzan-o-grams, strip-o-grams and lap dancers are usually more traumatic than amusing, as the one leaving is frequently encouraged to come into close contact with said entertainer's dangly bits. Not surprising, then, that a number of people now prefer not to leave after all rather than have simulated sex up a pole with a dancer looking at her watch.

Nobody knows the trouble they've
seen – except you, of course.
Five reasons to hate …

Hypochondriacs

Reason One: Whenever you ask how they are, they like to tell you – in excruciating, mind-numbing detail. Yes, they're 'managing' their A–Z of conditions, though it could well be their last Ultimate School Disco Office Party. You can only dream.

Reason Two: They're experts in illness (or rather, illnesses) and are certainly not interested in your bog-standard complaints. Colds mutate into unpleasant, year-long 'viruses' – no one likes to inquire too deeply lest they be given another tour of their 'insides' to rival Professor Von Hagen's Body Worlds.

Reason Three: They love specialising in complaints that come in capital letters. A mention of Sick Office Syndrome sends them scurrying for their own hermetically sealed plastic body bags, while SAD brings on a flurry of light bulbs to rival Elaine Paige's dressing room.

Reason Four: Alternative medicine has been a real boon to them, adding to their available psychodramas. Their box of Bach Flower Remedies – marigold petals picked at full moon – gives an entirely new meaning to the concept of neurasthenia. Only don't tell them: they'll only add it to their list of symptoms.

Reason Five: They like to make a career of being ill at work with, much to colleagues' annoyance, little time off. They might wave pathetically but have the secret constitution of an ox. It's everybody else who's in a state of nervous collapse. Pass the Bach Flower Rescue Remedy.

All the news that's not fit to print.
Five reasons to hate …

Internal
Communications

Reason One: Everyone claims it makes or breaks companies. That's why they employ a team of so-called 'professionals', whose idea of successful communication is editing a staff newspaper that makes the North Korean Information Department seem a fountain of truth in comparison.

Reason Two: Your company is communicating so many exciting new initiatives to its staff – from Giving Birth Under the IT Help Desk and Work Life Strategies: Getting Married in the Atrium to Managing Your Personal Development Because Frankly No One Else Is Going To – just don't all rush.

Reason Three: We all know that any internal communications strategy is basically to inform staff how caring, unique and deeply wonderful your company is. The hope is that if this is repeated enough times it will stick somewhere, even if this is mainly in people's gullets.

Reason Four: For a really juicy piece of news most of us realistically rely on the Chief Executive's PA (knows who's had sex on blotters in the boardroom) or the receptionist (can describe the *Fatal Attraction* moment in detail with frequent replays). If desperate, there's always the person in the office kitchen (er, find out who used their banana-flavoured Complan).

Reason Five: Should a matter of major importance need to be communicated, it's left to an Away Day (staff reduced to screaming and third-degree burns after a morning's fire-walking) or a sales conference (staff too drunk to care). It's usual to let them know what will happen if sales don't improve and will the last person to leave the company please turn out the fluorescent lights.

Get ready for the big
serial killer questions.
Five reasons to hate …
Interviews

Reason One: Advice ranges from being yourself (not recommended for most of us) to pretending to be someone else (probably best for most of us provided it isn't Osama Bin Laden). Deep breathing exercises are recommended but not in front of the interviewer unless you're currently seeking exciting phone-sex career opportunities.

Reason Two: You're allowed to copy the body language and style of your interviewer, although this can be difficult if there's more than one person and you're not a multiple schizophrenic with a sideline in transvestism. It may be better to concentrate on your best goggle-eyed look, stare straight at the interviewer, though without looking too much like Shelley Duvall in that scene with Jack Nicholson in *The Shining*. Just a little too scary.

Reason Three: Interviewers like to come with a ready-prepared script, which includes disarming warm-up questions (what is your name?), information gathering (what is your cat's name?), red herrings (how would your cat feel about these?), and killer questions (how would you feel about these?). If an internal candidate is present, remember you're only there to give them a laugh by revealing embarrassing details about your personal life.

Reason Four: Signs that the interview isn't going well include: (a) interviewer asleep; (b) interviewee asleep; (c) interview plant wilting with boredom – and it's plastic.

Reason Five: If you get a second interview this is always a good sign and means the internal candidate has let herself down by refusing to talk about her line manager's sexual peccadilloes in sufficient detail for the panel.

Cheer up, they only want to be your friends.
Five reasons to hate …

Irritating Colleagues

Reason One: They always like to play back voicemail messages on maximum (we love hearing about unpleasant crotch infections Wembley Arena-style) or speak loudly into their mobile phones (they're having a Snack Pot for lunch – as if we didn't know).

Reason Two: They like to show us ten years' of holiday photos/ tell us what's in their sandwich today/reveal their perfect recall of all programmes on UK Gold/have only ever read one book and, yes, it's *The Da Vinci Code*.

Reason Three: They make a big effort to be as depressing and unhelpful as possible by never saying good morning or doing the tea or coffee round, always putting two-pence pieces into leaving-present envelopes and having a general Dot Cotton-just-been-offered-a-nicotine-patch demeanour.

Reason Four: They always claim to be too busy or important to report a broken photocopier or fax, refill empty paper trays or take away photocopying. As for managers who can't operate any office equipment, please attend a 'Living In The Real World: Module One For Beginners – Pressing the Switch' training course and pronto.

Reason Five: On Planet Ideal Me, no one's game plan ever actually intended them to spend 24/7 breathing in their co-workers' dead skin cells. But it's still no excuse to scream at computers as if it they can actually hear us and then break down in gratitude when they work again. Sad or very sad?

Beware all ye who enter here.
Five reasons to hate …

Kitchens, Office

Reason One: Middle-class people who hang up their latte whisks in alphabetical order at home behave like slobs in office kitchens. They own cups with harrowing stains, leave puddles on the floor and steal milk using euphemisms such as 'borrowing'. Their unfinished Snack Pots and rust-encrusted trays with pictures of Edwardian Country Ladies make Mrs Royle's kitchen look like a Philippe Starck interior.

Reason Two: The office fridge offers deep and disturbing insights into your colleagues' lives: the person who lives off frozen Crunchies, the obsessive yoghurt eater, the owner of a pre-prepared bowl of Chicken Complan that they always leave next to your lunch. Office microwaves have a comparable status to public toilets, judging by what goes in them and how often they're cleaned.

Reason Three: Cleaners declare it a no-go area at departmental meetings and feel able to tell senior managers that they and their staff are dirty pigs. Everyone agrees but does nothing until someone finally snaps and makes a lunge for all the festering china and cutlery and throws them into the sink. This accounts for the mysterious number of mugs without handles in office kitchens.

Reason Four: Guests are forbidden entry lest they have a Martin Parr moment and see the cracked mug with its owner's initials in nail varnish, plus matching lipstick stains, that says 'Kylie Minogue: The Neighbours Tour 1987'. Also known as the guest's mug.

Reason Five: It's the room the feng shui consultant – not to mention the office architect – forgot: the poky space with off-white Formica where co-workers, squashed into proximity closer than the Northern Line, worry about being accused of sexual harassment. Try not to notice that memento mori row of ex-colleagues' mugs left gloatingly behind, together with their three-month-old half-eaten vegetable lasagnes.

If you don't hear from us, assume
we're still laughing at your CV.
Five reasons to hate …
Job Ads

Reason One: We all know about 'salary negotiable' (much less than you might think), 'excellent travel opportunities' (sub-branch in Wolverhampton), and 'all the advantages of a big organisation' (no one knows anyone else's name). But we wish they'd do something about 'you must be a creative person' (telling imaginative lies to MD's wife). We fall for it every time.

Reason Two: If you're over 45, you'll know not to apply for 'a high-energy post on the cutting edge of technology' and appreciate that advising customers about avocado bathroom suites in B&Q better suits your particular skills set.

Reason Three: If you're under 25, you won't want to miss 'a super opportunity for a first jobber!', i.e. you obviously have no discernible skills apart from having essay crises and listening to Coldplay so thank us for offering you this brilliant opportunity to enter the real world. You should be paying us.

Reason Four: Job ads like to give the impression that everyone else's job is much more glamorous and better paid than our own. When even chartered accountancy seems more attractive than your own job, it may be best to seek professional help.

Reason Five: In certain industries recruiters are allowed to specify posts for male or female applicants only, but there are also other areas where you can end up being the 'token woman' or 'token man'. You'll either be welcomed for your 'emotional intelligence' (can actually speak and listen) or they'll be pleased they've finally got someone to unblock the sink.

Look, if it makes you feel better, you can call yourself Mr Blobby.
Five reasons to hate …

Job Titles

Reason One: 'Bright and eager all-rounder' is the new Girl Friday who gets to do all the awful jobs for lousy money; 'PA' is the new secretary who's still searching for the paperless office; and 'executary' is the new senior secretary who at least has a feelgood name for doing her boss's job if nothing else. Plus câ change …

Reason Two: Human Resources used to be the chap from Personnel who did nice things with the Pensioners' Club. Now more likely to test you on the company's continuous improvement policy and to recommend you for psychometric assessment if you giggle when someone mentions Quality in meetings.

Reason Three: Someone has to be responsible for Britain having one of the lowest productivity rates in the Western world and for never knowing how to make a cup of coffee – they're called managers. They like to award themselves bizarre appellations like 'Knowledge Manager' – er, keeping twenty years of meeting minutes no one wants to read – to make everyone else feel incompetent or just plain confused.

Reason Four: Almost anyone can be an MD or chief executive. Half the MDs and chief execs in Britain were post-dotcom failures, who wore those funny black glasses and worked in their parents' back bedrooms in Basingstoke, seriously believing they were about to rule the world.

Reason Five: Consultants are often people too young and inexperienced to have proper jobs – which is why their reports have to be written in ur-management speak to warn people who might otherwise think their conclusions have any remote connection with the real world.

Something must be keeping you there.
Only you know what it is.
Five reasons to hate …

Knowing You've Been There Too Long

Reason One: You're the unofficial company induction course leader and every new person is told to ask you about: (a) the degree of vomiting required for credible fake sickie; (b) how many hours of illegal internet use are possible on a normal working day; (c) how many office toys are allowed before it's assumed you're having a nervous breakdown. At least someone appreciates you.

Reason Two: Your boss can't fool you any more with their management jargon: you know all about 'staff development' (you take on so many extra responsibilities, you don't have time to work out that your salary hasn't gone up) and 're-structuring' (other staff made redundant and most of their work and stress problems are passed to you).

Reason Three: Your job descriptions have grown to include Seer (knows where the only plate in the entire organisation is kept), Futurologist (knows from experience how long the latest management trend will last), and Wise Person (knows when to give in and put buying the MD's wedding anniversary present under 'multi-tasking').

Reason Four: Let's face it, the office Christmas party wouldn't be the same without you. Who else is going to locate a hundred Donna Summer glitter wigs and make sure the singing Santa-gram exposes himself to a visiting client as usual?

Reason Five: Gloating ex-colleagues like to return – and let you know they have much better jobs than you. The last time you seriously job searched, everyone was worrying about the future of the mullet and you wanted to marry Andrew Ridgley. Er, maybe time for a serious rethink?

Having second thoughts about going now? We can't think why. Five reasons to hate …

Leaving Parties

Reason One: Does anyone appreciate the impact of frequent job-hopping and a Scrooge-like workforce on the poor person designated leaving-present collector and shopper? And what about the problem of finding a Clinton card to match the leaver's personality – it's nice to know you can best be summed up by a picture of a suicidal Eeyore.

Reason Two: It's the worst kept secret since the eviction of George Galloway – senior PAs are observed for days attempting to hide bulging envelopes in handbags, while most of the company is in the lavatory signing your Tweenies card. Just hope they don't bulk up your presents with discounted client Christmas gifts. Gosh, you've always wanted a miniature set of prune liquors.

Reason Three: It's your leaving party and you can cry if you want to, but don't kid anybody you aren't really leaving for better things elsewhere. And don't be fooled: your colleagues' crying isn't a show of unsuspected affection – they're just bloody jealous.

Reason Four: It's too cursory just to say goodbye, while a full-blown Bacchanalia unfortunately may not be allowed. So a compromise is often reached with a piece of cake and a visit to the local pub. Just don't smirk: everyone knows the company will save several months' salary by not reappointing immediately and expecting everyone else to do your work.

Reason Five: You should try to look surprised at your leaving party, as if all you ever expected to receive was your P45. Tell them what a wonderful work place it's been (that's why you're leaving), what a lot of friends you've made (most of those here are freeloaders), and how spooky it is them knowing your obsession with Captain Scarlet bath products.

Will the last person out of
the door please remember
not to feel guilty for once.
Five reasons to hate …

Long Hours

Reason One: Everyone feels guilty about leaving on time and resorts to various lies and excuses. These include: (a) doing your best Winona Ryder impersonation – 'this is the first time I've ever done it and it won't happen again'; (b) leaving a particularly nasty jacket on your chair – although people will feel sorry for your pathetic attempts at presenteeism and there'll be rumours that you've got a home life.

Reason Two: Company gyms, dry cleaners, beauticians, florists, travel agents – but why stop there? Expect to be in a Japanese-style, two-by-two-metre sleeping-pod soon if your HR team has anything to do with it.

Reason Three: More and more of our relationships are apparently the direct result of meeting a co-worker. This isn't surprising really when many of us don't meet anyone else apart from late-night garage-shop assistants. You've probably watched your prospective partner in screaming negotiation mode so you'll know what to expect over breakfast.

Reason Four: If you're a woman with children, it means not having a life; if you're her partner, it just means having a good excuse for not doing any childcare and sometimes being late for football.

Reason Five: Isn't going out with colleagues for after-work drinks just a sad extension of the office, but just involving more sick on the floor? Even sadder when you realise your line-manager is there and the rest of your character assassination and filthiest joke have to be saved for your imminent leaving party.

Look, whatever it is, it's
your fault, OK?
Five reasons to hate ...

Making Mistakes

Reason One: Ever noticed how no one ever makes mistakes apart from you? That's because your colleagues are experienced bull-shitters. They know that by admitting to the most minor misdeeds – 'sorry, I might have forgotten to refill the photocopier', 'I was guilty of over-watering the plant' – no one will suspect them of losing the company millions.

Reason Two: Facing accusers in a meeting, the expert bull-shitter will always deflect blame onto others. This could involve 'we' (the team), 'We' (the company), 'Them' (the Government) or 'Him' (Bill Gates or God). And there's always someone present who can have their character denigrated – 'er, I won't talk about him behind his back' (don't worry, I know I can leave that to the rest of you).

Reason Three: Of course it helps if you're the MD or the Chief Executive – even if you bring your company close to bankruptcy, you'll still get a £300,000 pay-off and a discreet six-month exit strategy. No one wants to admit they made a big mistake hiring you. It seems likely that your current perma-tanned and multi-homed state will continue for some time to come.

Reason Four: If you work in public services, the blame culture ensures that many spend their entire careers blaming other people and with big organisations this can last for decades. The government now encourages whistle-blowers to come in and try to keep everyone awake.

Reason Five: Don't worry, there's always someone they can blame for: (a) corporate collapse; (b) failed management; (c) global warming. Well volunteered – you always knew it was in your job description.

At least you've got somebody
else useless to blame.
Five reasons to hate …
Management

Reason One: Real offices, real salaries and real people to do all the work for them – and they think they're stressed. Ever notice how, when company news is good it's due to their strategic brilliance. When it's bad – and you're being made redundant – it's nothing to do with them.

Reason Two: Lots of idiotic jargon, e.g. 'helicopter vision' (basically out of control at dangerous elevation and expect to crash land shortly), 'managing expectations' (especially when it comes to your salary increase; don't forget the wide range of benefits we give you including a chair and a vestigial lunch break), and 'continuous improvement' (with particular reference to their increased salaries naturally).

Reason Three: Oh dear, all those embarrassing theories that were supposed to revolutionise the workplace – from re-engineering (companies apparently don't need any employees) to Japanese-style management (everyone doing sushi for lunch until Japanese economy flounders). Surely some mistake?

Reason Four: 'Er, basically your job is crap and poorly paid with ridiculously long hours, but to make you think we're consensual and caring we're going to provide you with someone to massage your feet the wrong way.' At least you know where you are with managers who just remove your cubicle.

Reason Five: Whether they're leading team building in Tenerife or Thinking the Impossible (what am I getting paid for?), ask yourself if the absence of management would make the slightest bit of difference to the current trajectory of your company. Those wanting a reference will probably keep it from them until their tired and emotional leaving-party speech.

And maybe pigs will fly.
Five reasons to hate …

Managing Change

Reason One: More jobs for the consultants or just a way to keep employees permanently on Diareze? No one's quite sure if your friendly change manager is simply there to help you sort out your new desk arrangement. Or is he really about ensuring there are enough skips when the next budget cuts are announced?

Reason Two: Sorry, we know they're nice people but don't Human Resources now see their role as more like hard-faced change implementers? Don't they care that soon there'll be no one left to remind staff about their twenty-eight failed dress codes?

Reason Three: Know how much longer you've got by your company's change management strategy: (a) a change manager means they're thinking longer term – at least you can have a nice, long nervous breakdown in public; (b) a change consultant means redundancies are imminent; (c) a change awareness workshop means they'll bring in an arts-based trainer, who'll use *Hamlet* to help you cope with the likely scenario (i.e., you're dead).

Reason Four: Don't be fooled: admittedly, 'hey, there's a transformational process of change going on and you're right at the interface of it' sounds better than 'you're fired' or 'your security pass is no longer valid'. But only just.

Reason Five: Nobody's ever seen the team so busy at their PCs. Chiefly because everyone's manically updating their CVs, checking job sites, and making arrangements for safe removal of any personal evidence that you might once have ever existed – a last-minute rush is so Enron.

It's the only way you'll ever get to sleep
with your entire department.
Five reasons to hate ...

Meetings

Reason One: If the minutes of meetings were accurately recorded, they'd be a cross between a Virginia Woolf stream-of-consciousness novel (your boss), The Neverending Story (his boss), and The Invisible Man (you). No wonder we like to have them behind closed doors.

Reason Two: They last so long the meeting room's like a second home – except you don't generally go for a Spearmint Rhino look with paper cups and mini-Bounty wrappers everywhere. A weak chairman and a few individuals who've seen Michael Douglas in *Wall Street* are all that's needed to make sure listening to others is kept to a minimum – just as well considering the number of people in the early stages of REM.

Reason Three: An increasing number are scheduled at ridiculous times. The breakfast meeting sees everyone desperately trying to say something intelligent to the Chief Executive ('Can you pass the Cornflakes, please?'), while the evening meeting sees a mixture of resignation ('there doesn't seem much point in going home') and starvation ('can I have half your Polo?'). Partners ring continually about dinner – the meeting temporarily abandoned each time as people mouth to each other that 'it's in the dog'.

Reason Four: If you're a woman and the tea trolley arrives, there's every chance you'll have to be 'mother'. Centuries of conditioning means that the male drive flags at the first sign of a steaming pot, while pouring is seen as the next best thing to cross-dressing in front of colleagues.

Reason Five: The staff association meeting can't be anything but acrimonious, as no one working in an office ever feels their true needs are being met. Management reps – 'I think you'll find we're doing everything to meet your vestigial rights, legally speaking, and not every kitchen has a sink like ours' – will put you in the picture pretty quickly.

Should you be relieved or worried that he only ever speaks to you in the toilet? Five reasons to hate …

Meeting the Chief Executive

Reason One: If he ignores you in the corridor, you feel devastated. If he calls you by someone else's name, you think you have the personality of an amoeba. If he remembers your name, you assume you must be on the next redundancy hit list. No, you can't win.

Reason Two: If he speaks to you in the toilet at the next urinal, you're faced with a number of etiquette dilemmas. Do you finish after him? Do you finish at the same time? Or do you frankly feel it's the ultimate boys' trip to be discussing global penetration with both your penises hanging out, and try your best to take it seriously?

Reason Three: If you find yourself in the lift with him, you have a maximum of twenty seconds to be seen as either desperate (act like a tongue-tied stalker and forget your own name) or very desperate (do your embarrassing Personal Elevator CV pitch without blushing).

Reason Four: At a conference, he'll offer you a limp handshake if you're in one of those 'shot at dawn' lines of shiny middle management suits. Otherwise it'll just be a *Where's Wally* crowd situation – except, sorry, no one's going to be looking for you, loser.

Reason Five: It's Sod's Law that you both get paired up on a 'Discovering Your Corporate Creative Person' Day. At least for the first time in your working lives you'll have something in common, apart from sheer terror, as you show everyone the toilet roll recreation of the internal communications vision you've made together. Don't be shy …

Of course they're not all going to be like David Brent, don't be silly.
Five reasons to hate …

Middle Managers

Reason One: The 'flattening of hierarchies' was supposed to have cut out this wasteful management layer. Only then along came *The Office*'s David Brent and everyone admitted to knowing someone just like him who achieves nothing and has done a motivational dance at a sales conference. Still some way to go then.

Reason Two: They're trapped between us and senior management and find themselves 'managing upwards' (letting their bosses know they're working the longest hours in the company and haven't had a family life since 1999), while the rest of us do their real jobs for them.

Reason Three: Over the last decade they've tried to give us plenty of support ('er, the chair is temporarily yours'). They've also offered us every new management theory going from Emotional Intelligence (at last something for the ladies) to Spiritual Intelligence (nothing else works, maybe prayers will).

Reason Four: Most middle managers like to see their management styles as macho (Gordon Gecko School of Management), leading by example (Battle of Balaclava School of Management), hands off (Rip Van Winkle School of Management) or New Age (David Icke School of Management). Normal work can usually be resumed as quickly as possible afterwards.

Reason Five: While we rarely get to see the Chief Executive, middle managers meet this person several times a year, always being very careful to 'manage expectations' (blame everything that goes wrong on someone else), 'think the unthinkable' (suggest they should be in line for the best promotion), and 'walk the talk' (actually have the nerve to go around saying all this crap).

Think of it as D-Day – er, as in
Depression Day, that is.
Five reasons to hate …

Monday Mornings

Reason One: From feeling our solar plexus on the No.19 bus without being arrested, to deep breathing like a Wes Craven soundtrack – the job doc's 'feel-good' techniques just don't work. As for making other days 'the new Monday' by doing all our horrid jobs in advance, please, when else do they think we're going to get any proper sleeping done?

Reason Two: We briefly forgot what it was like to be in close proximity to other people's body fluids in a space even David Blaine would've found cramped. Is it just our imaginations or is public transport more obscenely full on Monday mornings as the compulsive sickie brigade avoid an obvious long weekend?

Reason Three: Don't even think about the water-cooler TV conversations you're going to hear – the *Antiques Roadshow*, an historical drama, and repeats of repeats of *Last Of The Summer Wine*. Please, don't make us even more suicidal.

Reason Four: Today is the first day of the rest of your life – except you don't want to spend the rest of your life in a chip-board cubicle with colleagues who wish to rap about Susan Hampshire or their wet Sunday afternoon in a Homebase.

Reason Five: 'What fresh hell is this?' said Dorothy Parker, and she didn't even have to go straight into a three-hour Monday morning meeting with people whose idea of fun is adding up their work competencies over the weekend. They're just very lucky you can be there.

You'll live the brand but you're not hugging the woman from Accounts, OK?
Five reasons to hate …
Motivators

Reason One: They're always an admission of management incompetence brought in as a last resort – though they like to claim it as a brilliant piece of strategic thinking, i.e. passing the buck to someone else because they haven't a clue what to do next.

Reason Two: The company is sufficiently anxious to involve everybody – though with much concern that, come the big day, some staff may not know how to wear M&S elasticised trousers or look resigned when the flip chart collapses yet again.

Reason Three: The motivator will always be American. Having someone who hasn't travelled 3000 miles just to tell us how to smile at customers will be seen as grossly insulting. 'Feeling your Inner Brand and Bringing Joy to the Customer Interface' by a man from Leatherhead is just asking for collective narcolepsy.

Reason Four: Your motivator will want to resort to (a) testimonials – there was a time in distant history when they weren't millionaires; (b) incentives – they give you a dollar bill because it sounds more aspirational than fifty pence; (c) dancing – doing Dad Dancing at 10 am to unlock your chakras; (d) embracing your neighbour – after the Dad Dancing you need as much support as you can get.

Reason Five: Everybody now knows what it is to be motivated by one's job and can see what is missing in their life – in most cases a visit to the recruitment website of their choice at the earliest opportunity.

What do they expect you to do,
give it away?
Five reasons to hate …
Negotiating

Reason One: We all know to be aware of the other side's strengths and weaknesses as well as our own bottom line – which in our case usually means crying in a public place and having a complete stranger lend us a tissue, call us duck and give us our bus fare home.

Reason Two: Success depends on understanding: (a) stages of negotiation – always having something up our sleeves we don't mind giving away, like ten years' worth of unread office computer manuals; (b) they already have them and don't know what to do with them either; (c) styles of influence – basically, will we be doing a Robert de Niro 'are you looking at me?' special or going more for a *Coronation Street*, Hayley Patterson 'I always wanted to be a human doormat'?

Reason Three: Negotiating with a client over a meal means remembering that we're a representative of our company, making it essential to have a chocolate mocha moustache, choke on rocket salad and have Halloween spinach teeth at all times.

Reason Four: It's important to understand different sorts of contracts including those: (a) written on napkins (recognised in every Italian restaurant); (b) written in blood (recognised in certain Italian restaurants); (c) written in water (usually discovered back in the office).

Reason Five: Closing the deal is the most important part of negotiating when our body language lets our opponent know we have reached our Last Chance Saloon moment and could throw in an espresso and a lemon sorbet if that helps.

If people just advertised jobs, it'd save us an awful lot of varicose veins.
Five reasons to hate …

Networking

Reason One: Talking to strangers is always a nightmare, which is why some like to take a tip out of the chuggers' book and rudely interrupt conversations, telling people you're representing the poor, i.e. yourself. At least it's true and you should get some kind of response. This can range from social ostracism to strange facial tics.

Reason Two: At any typical networking event you can expect to pick up business cards from life coaches, counsellors, Reiki healers, cognitive behaviour therapists and a woman who always looks like Carole Caplin, plus sixteen napkins, two doilies and a beer mat – all of which may convince you it's perhaps better for the time being to remain in your existing job.

Reason Three: Speed networking just increases the number of bouncy castle business cards you're likely to receive in half an hour. Think about it.

Reason Four: It's supposed to help if you email everyone you spoke to, thanking them for their help and reminding them you were the person who interrupted their conversation and brought it round to one of the most interesting and burning topics of the day, i.e. yourself. They're bound to remember you.

Reason Five: You're supposed to network even if you aren't desperate for a job as, so the theory goes, you never know who might be useful on your way up – or down. This is especially the case if your highest-profile connections are currently the person from Accounts who says nice things about your carrier bag, and someone from IT trying for an NVQ Level 1 in Basic Social Skills.

Party, party, party – please try
to look more excited.
Five reasons to hate …

Office Christmas
Party, The

Reason One: You wish the office Christmas party had never happened. You're still wondering if: (a) a grope that lasts twenty seconds can be accurately described as a sexual relationship; (b) the pokey room with all the broken PCs is used at any other time of year; (c) direct eye contact will ever be resumed again in your department.

Reason Two: The MD pops in for his annual minimal-contact staff-bonding exercise, thanks you for all your 'throughput', and explains why there's no bonus this year. But someone's put a pair of flashing antlers on your head, so at least he'll remember you.

Reason Three: You've already heard the Christmas small talk of your colleagues ten times over, which seems to consist of transporting relatives no one likes from one front room to an identical one on the other side of the country. If you hear about how busy Boots is again you'll scream.

Reason Four: Everyone is so aware of the possible tacky connotations that, come the Big Day, colleagues avoid direct eye contact, the photocopier is strictly out of bounds and the lap dancer complains she isn't being sexually harassed.

Reason Five: Once the glitter from the office Christmas party has settled, the post-party analysis begins. It's seen as too corporate (company business plan in crackers), just plain boring (person seated next to the woman from Procurement), or thematically confused (lap dancer in Victorian bonnet).

Remember, whatever it is you're doing, somebody else can do it more cheaply.
Five reasons to hate …

Outsourcing

Reason One: On the basis of a management theory from a crazed right-wing professor in Nebraska, the Chief Executive wants to know which departments' work could be done more cheaply elsewhere. No one's job is safe from outsourcing apart from outsourcing consultants who spend their time asking questions like: why shouldn't your job be performed by unqualified people who cost less so the resultant savings pay for their exorbitant fees?

Reason Two: Soon it's like a Big Brother vote – from Marketing (we could sell fridge magnets to Innuits) and Finance (but we'd put them on ice floes if they didn't pay up) to the woman who cleans telephones (I give good disinfectant), no one is immune from humiliating themselves to prove they shouldn't be outsourced.

Reason Three: The public sector once thought it didn't dare copy these private sector practices, then along came 'Public–Private Partnerships', i.e. we don't actually want to call it outsourcing but it's alright now we've come up with a poncy new name with capital letters.

Reason Four: It's only a matter of time before the outplacement advisor is brought in to suggest various alternatives for you, which always include becoming: (a) an aromatherapist; (b) a life coach; (c) an outplacement advisor.

Reason Five: So many people are leaving that the girl who secretly organises leaving presents is buying twenty crop tops and novelty boxer shorts at any one time – and there are rumours Secret Santa will be run from a call centre in Western Indonesia and all the presents will be George Foreman sandwich grills.

Don't worry, we think you're a genius.
Five reasons to hate being …

Overqualified

Reason One: To gain employment, a large percentage of graduates have to claim they can't wait to: (a) photocopy; (b) make tea; (c) hear all about how their boss was educated at 'the school of life and didn't read a book until he was forty-two and look at him now, Sonny Jim'. After all, no one wishes to be thought above their work station in life.

Reason Two: With more and more of us having degrees, our bosses like to make the most of our academic skills, from Drama (straight into the call centre) and Geography (won't need to buy them a Sat Nav then) to History (should remember a few birthdays) and Media Studies (at least someone'll know how to operate the DVD player). A-level entrants know to break down at an even earlier stage.

Reason Three: Entrants in so-called 'glamorous' sectors from TV to publishing are nearly always massively overqualified. But when asked why they're filing all day for rubbish money, they know to reply that even Abi Titmuss had to wear some clothes at an early stage in her career.

Reason Four: Managers prefer to recruit team members with fewer qualifications than themselves for fear people will soon realise that running a department based on the pivotal texts of *The Rats* and *The Bourne Supremacy* may leave them open to some criticism.

Reason Five: Many women working part time are over-qualified but know that companies prefer them to develop their 'soft skills' chiefly in areas where men are proven genetically incapable, such as remembering birthdays, pouring tea at meetings and washing the department's only J-Cloth on a bi-annual basis.

Only another 346 days to go.
We know.
Five reasons to hate …

Post-Holiday Blues

Reason One: A fortnight away and your tolerance for stained carpet tiles and walnut melamine veneer is at an all-time low. It doesn't help either that: (a) in your absence you've been volunteered for every boring task going – we hope you like Health and Safety meetings about dangerous paper towel dispensers; (b) someone has been using your desk for an unknown purpose involving a sticky substance; (c) colleagues are breathing a sigh of relief that they don't have to pretend to do your work any more.

Reason Two: Please, we all know we're supposed to spend the first day back easing slowly into the daily grind, except no one explained this to our boss or the global economy or the senders of 987 emails we haven't answered. Funny this.

Reason Three: We all know that any euphoria lasts for approximately ten minutes before a colleague asks us if we realise that our summer holiday has come at the most inconvenient time of the year (i.e. the summer), and another won't believe us when we say we didn't secretly take her new stapler to Sri Lanka and bury it on the beach.

Reason Four: Experts suggest expensive spa breaks, beauty treatments and spiritual teachers to prolong the 'holiday halo' effect but this requires 'post-holiday' money. All most of us can manage is that essential mantra: 'If that woman asks about her stapler again I shall scream!'

Reason Five: It's amazing how quickly all those dreams of converting a ruined chateau or running your own business dissolve as soon as you get the next credit card bill. You stare at the postcard you sent to your colleagues and wonder if wearing a felt national costume and dancing in hotel foyers could be a viable career alternative.

Unaccustomed as you are
to public squeaking.
Five reasons to hate …

Presentations

Reason One: Management like us to think anyone can do it. How many times, after all, have you held colleagues spellbound with your theory of what a jar of Vaseline is doing in the sales manager's office? At office parties, haven't workmates lauded you as the next Roy 'Chubby' Brown? Presentations are apparently just a simple matter of transferring these essential skills to Quality System ISO 9000.

Reason Two: Read from a script and you might as well issue audiences with airline snooze slippers and a 1981 Goldie Hawn movie. Using simple key words on cards as triggers is fine unless you get them out of order and you find yourself doing your startling, new one-person William Burroughs 'cut-up collage' show.

Reason Three: Being relentlessly on message is the number one rule, but not if the sound bite is 'spreadsheet analysis' repeated 38 times, please.

Reason Four: No matter what they say, you'll be nervous. Trainers tell you simply to visualise all the members of your audience totally naked. After all, that's what most of them are going to be doing to you, unless they're already counting your pores on the giant overhead plasma screen or mouthing Visible Panty Line, that is.

Reason Five: Whatever can go wrong technologically will. If you're doing a PowerPoint presentation, you'll be certain to accidentally include that film your friend sent you of robots dancing in Hawaiian grass skirts. Always expect overhead sheets to melt and offer a startlingly authentic, 1968, psychedelic-show experience. Ditto if your interactive graphics software package breaks down and you end up having to do all the frolicking pie charts and funny voices yourself.

Prove how ideally suited you are
to corporate life. Or not.
Five reasons to hate …
Psychometric
Testing

Reason One: Is it really fair that Hannah in Human Resources now knows more about your innermost thought processes and personality quirks than your partner? Who does she think she is: God or something? Actually, yes ...

Reason Two: Well, are you an extrovert ('I see my closest rival as Jim Davidson'), agreeable ('Julie Andrews was always my childhood icon'), or a team player ('I never wanted to be an individual, honest')? Of course not. That's why you're practising like mad How To Be a New Model Worker on the 'Stepford Employee Personality Test' website.

Reason Three: Sadly, being rated 'bootylicious' by your speed internet dater won't impress the assessors. The Myers-Briggs Personality Type Indicator is much more interested in how dull and efficient you can be in most corporate situations. Zzzzzzz.

Reason Four: Such a shame you can't find your wonderful personality traits in any of the tests. Still, we're sure your colleagues will give you the benefit of their character assassinations – sorry, assessments – especially if you linger behind them at the water cooler.

Reason Five: Just when it seemed too many of us had got the hang of the interview technique and karaoke body language, they decide to drag us off to assessment centres for extra torture. The Coffee Stain Test For Predicting Deviant Office Kitchen Behaviour, anyone? About the only assessment we'll ever pass with flying colours.

Are there fairies at the bottom
of your garden, too?
Five reasons to hate …
Public-Private
Partnerships

Reason One: If you're in the public sector, you're terrified that a bunch of profit-mad, downsizing-crazy, in-thrall-to-share-holders, fast-buck companies will have you working after 5 pm. If you're in the private sector, you can't believe the death-by-committee, bloated bureaucracies. Lots to look forward to, then.

Reason Two: If you're in the public sector, expect to see changes to your 1970s death-by-falling-concrete office soon. According to the government, it's the only way to get some badly needed money into your sector. But while each side may see the other as either *Jaws* or *The Life of Dinosaurs*, the end result is more like *Pearl Harbour* – the director's cut.

Reason Three: People think partnerships are easy – all you need is a logo and Margaret Beckett reading from an autocue. But the world is full of failed partnerships – think one in four marriages or Geri Halliwell and your patience.

Reason Four: It's had more spin than *The Magic Roundabout*. New Labour loves it. Old Labour hates it. The Tories would like even more of it – how about Richard Desmond to run the Arts Council and getting Andrew Motion to write for *Nuts*?

Reason Five: The London Transport public-private partnership is signed, sealed and delivered. We'll just have to wait and see. Probably for 30 minutes at Baker Street with an overhead message no one can understand.

All those hours you spent downloading
essays off the internet.
Five reasons to hate ...
Qualifications

Reason One: MBAs. The only people in Britain who know the difference between a vision statement and a mission statement – or even care. But don't be jealous: you've probably had an MBM (Masters in Business Multi-Tasking, from running the company to making the coffee) for much longer.

Reason Two: Degrees. Congratulations, you've spent three years of your life to advertise to your employer that you're basically numerate (Maths), literate (English), a good little note-taker (History), or don't mind people making jokes about you (Media Studies).

Reason Three: Professional qualifications. It always sounds impressive if weird acronyms no one understands take up half a page of your CV – knowing that you're a QTM (certified Quality Tea-Bag Manager) is bound to impress lots of people.

Reason Four: A levels. If you've got an arts one, the chances are you managed to hold a York Notes the right way up. If you've got a science one, at least you'll have some basic theory for the early stages of pukka pie decomposition in the office micro-wave.

Reason Five: GCSEs. Er, has acquired basic office skills of sitting in a room for two years, texting and chatting about latest soap episodes. Well, it's more than half the Royal Family have got, look at it like that.

Their ideal job for you is always the one nobody else wants.
Five reasons to hate …

Recruitment Agencies

Reason One: Please, everyone knows it's only a temporary job that a chimpanzee with no brain could do, so they needn't pretend that it's nuclear physics in disguise or that working in a road near Oxford Street makes it impossibly glamorous. Honestly, if we were really that concerned we'd get ourselves a proper job.

Reason Two: We know they're very keen to place us in that exciting job in finances but we've told them on a number of occasions that we think a spreadsheet is something you find on the ground floor of John Lewis. Not so much transferable skills then as total meltdown.

Reason Three: We never actually get to meet because everything's virtual but does this matter, as they seem genetically programmed to assume that women can do anything with typing or filing, and that any fashion job is automatically creative and won't just be glorified spell-checking for people who can't spell 'pretentious'. Moi?

Reason Four: We know they carefully screen and vet all us job applicants, but it would help if employers could be likewise screened so that if we have to sit in an office all day doing nothing and being avoided by everyone we can at least be informed at an earlier stage.

Reason Five: We know that many of the so-called 'exceptional' and 'once-in-a-lifetime' jobs on their books are ones that no one in their right mind would want to do, and offering us a free biro isn't, sadly, going to make a great deal of difference. Break it to them gently.

We believe you – unfortunately
others are having trouble.
Five reasons to hate …
References

Reason One: 'Lively' (shouts down the phone); 'confident' (answers back); 'pleasant personality' (too thick for words); 'creative' (doodles on invoices); 'good telephone manner' (inane and upper class). Nobody believes them, of course, but after your CV and interview, why stop at the foothills when you can scale Everest? Someone's got to keep the global economy ticking over, after all.

Reason Two: References are a minefield for employers and many now give out simple statements: 'X sat at a desk on and off for Y number of years in front of a computer' may be the only factually correct piece of information about you, but at least it won't raise too many ridiculous expectations.

Reason Three: Is your boss really going to want to say goodbye to the person who does all his crap jobs and knows his wife's lingerie measurements? It's probably better to ask the nice woman in HR who strokes your Flump if she won't mind giving you a fulsome little encomium that'll leave her just this side of gagging.

Reason Four: If you can pre-empt a potentially damaging reference ('and then a fabricated print of my erect penis and buttocks was, so they claimed, removed from the photocopier …'), there's a good chance your next employer will still offer you the job and only want to show it to a select group of your future colleagues.

Reason Five: If no one in your company will give you a reference, there's always Stan the Man in your local pub who can vouch for your status as a trustworthy and caring person – just make sure he gets your name right.

It's your cubicle and you can
cry if you want to.
Five reasons to hate …
Sad Behaviour

Reason One: An office rearrangement doesn't mean you have to break down because: (a) you're further from a window and this is a major slight to your job description; (b) your files have been temporarily mislaid; (c) your Day-Glo Care Bear has been squashed and declared inoperable. Just think about world poverty or even get a life.

Reason Two: Just because you're unmarried, over 30 and following the latest self-help dating strategy doesn't mean you have to attend every IT meeting in the hope of encountering the maximum number of men or, pretending to be Kim Cattrall in *Sex and the City*, give out cups at the water cooler to anyone in Y-fronts.

Reason Three: Screaming at your PC and threatening to annihilate it off the face of the earth, and then making orgasmic, cooing noises because it has accepted your new instructions, suggests you may take checking a few emails a little too seriously.

Reason Four: Er, it's not very sensible coming to work dressed as a giant panda or turkey, or wearing hot pants for a day to support your favourite charity if no one else knows about it. Just put the collection bucket over your head and pretend not to be there, please.

Reason Five: Most of us find ourselves reverting to type in the office kitchens by keeping vintage sandwiches in the fridge and leaving our 'Cliff: The Musical' mug for others to wash up – or else displaying curt little notices to announce our displeasure at such behaviour. You don't have to be sad to work here, but it helps.

Give up – they have ways of making sure you're humiliated.
Five reasons to hate …

Sales Conferences

Reason One: Rival companies whisk their staff off to Malta or Marbella for a long weekend of sun, sea and a little light Power-Point. Yours prefers anywhere within choking distance of the M25: Thurrock, Slough, Watford and Croydon are all hot spots.

Reason Two: Essential ingredients for a tumultuous time include a hotel offering a Recessionary Special (share a room and bring your own UHT milk), artistic displays of muesli, a receptionist selling tartan soft toys in case you need something to play with, and line-dancing senior citizens in the room next door. But look enthusiastic at all times: your job depends on it.

Reason Three: Most people in the Tony Orlando Conference Room are either tense (they've got something to do) or asleep (they haven't). Your MD opens with the most ecstatic speech you're likely to hear this side of the Mount of Olives. Once VIPs have exited, reps are informed that if sales don't improve they'll be back in Mondeos and their Garfields will be confiscated.

Reason Four: Remember, a sales conference isn't worth its name if unsuitable, introverted members of staff aren't required to perform in front of everyone to enliven boring sales stories. That's you, that is.

Reason Five: In order to promote corporate bonding, management forces you to attend the dinner from hell where you sit next to a conversationally restricted sanitary engineer and all you can do is discuss blockages and what's in the crème brulée. Don't worry, alcohol is banned.

Why does everyone seem to be having it apart from you?
having it apart from you?
Five reasons to hate …

Sex in the Office

Reason One: Even if X and Y are doing it they: (a) never arrive together; (b) keep a cool, professional distance in the office; (c) don't see every day as an excuse for priapic behaviour, unlike everyone else in your department who can't visit a photocopier or stationery cupboard without the need for a lewd comment.

Reason Two: They're probably not even among the ten per cent who claim to be having regular desk-toppling office sex. But where the latter are having it in our unappealing offices is a mystery to most of us. Broom cupboards? Fire exits? Under their desk during meetings? Sad and/or presumably very fluffy.

Reason Three: We all have an Emma in Accounts who accidentally sends details of her and Darren's 'love knobs' to all of the leaders of the G8 countries and finds this quite amusing. But more than once is an Obsessive Compulsive Disorder and everyone asks Emma to please put her increasingly tiresome 'love knobs' back where they belong.

Reason Four: When you can apparently get it every day, it makes The Last Days of the Roman Empire that was the office Christmas party seem hardly worth wearing that Frosty the Snowman prosthesis for. Is this the end of the MD's annual pole-dance as we know it?

Reason Five: Everyone is so aware of the possible flaky implications of sales conferences that hotel room keys are fumbled with at record speed. No one says goodnight lest they be accused of sexual harassment. And everyone watches an animal documentary alone for the rest of the evening and gets put off the idea completely anyway.

Phew, at least there's someone else they can criticise now. Five reasons to hate …

Smokers, Attitudes to

Reason One: Those weird, embarrassed groups of people huddled outside office entrances wondering what to do with their stubs and looking like unofficial 1970s pickets – smokers are the new pariahs of the workplace. At least someone else, apart from you, can now be given patronising lectures.

Reason Two: Smokers' rooms are a cross between Vilnius airport lounge circa 1978 and that scene in *Taxi Driver* where Robert De Niro drives above the steaming New York sewers and we're supposed to think it's Hell. They don't actually want smokers to live much longer. Nice, then.

Reason Three: Smokers are criticised for having combined coffee and cigarette breaks to say nasty, intense things about their managers, as opposed to just coffee breaks. As if there's any real difference, except those having a fag are just standing in the cold on a fire escape on the twenty-ninth floor.

Reason Four: Spider plants – previously subjected to humane culling through use as ashtrays – have been given an extended life expectancy and are reaching epidemic proportions because of smoking-free offices.

Reason Five: It's back behind the bike sheds for the motley crew of office smokers. Pariah smoking brings together everyone, from distribution to directors, for regular corporate bonding over shared lighter situations. It's much cheaper than having an Away Day and really is the new Masons, except that everybody just coughs a lot more.

Just in case you thought you weren't
taking 24/7 seriously enough.
Five reasons to hate …
Socialising with Colleagues

Reason One: It suddenly strikes you that colleagues are the new relatives because: (a) you didn't choose them and you haven't got much in common; (b) they think you want to be with them 24/7; (c) they give you awful Christmas presents.

Reason Two: Here comes another fuggy, blurry evening in a bar or club themed specially for office workers: Ibiza (hoping to lose consciousness again very quickly); School Disco (you can't get enough of uniforms); 1980s (you can't get enough of Simon Le Bon); or Anthems (you like being in traffic jams on the M25).

Reason Three: It's always difficult if one of these colleagues happens to be your line manager. Is your participation in an all-round-the-venue, 'What all the Hoes Love' gangsta-rap conga seen as an example of teamwork or a sackable offence?

Reason Four: You can just about hack discussing business plans or strategies in the office, but not after work for several hours. You always knew you had nothing else in common: why can't they just sit and watch the ice-skating from Bulgaria on the screen like everyone else?

Reason Five: Don't worry, whatever your excuse, you won't be able to get out of Christmas (bring your own flashing Santa hat), birthdays (bring your own vomitorium), leaving parties (most tasteless person always chooses present), or redundancy parties (lap dancer wears P45). Ho, don't be such a spoil-sport!

Definitely a course for concern.
Five reasons to hate …
Staff Canteens

Reason One: Suddenly they're all getting trendy new names and coming to terms with the idea that human life is possible without congealed chips and unknown items freeze-dried in Taiwan in 1992. You definitely smell something fishy – or should we say *filet de poissons*.

Reason Two: Naturally, your company's not giving you a posh dining suite, bistro with 'theatre-style' cooking and coffee shop for nothing. They just want you to stay at work forever, thinking you're enjoying a dream lifestyle because you've got a fish knife. They know that otherwise you'll spend an 18-hour working day eating Hula Hoops and then die.

Reason Three: Sorry, eating all your meals there on a regular basis suggests: (a) you're a desperate networker – you think someone is going to say, 'hey, it's the new star of Outlook Express for Beginners, we want to groom her for stardom'; (b) no one in your department likes you; (c) you obviously don't have enough work to do.

Reason Four: It's one of those rare occasions when everyone in the company can bond – so it's as embarrassing as the office Christmas party, except usually with fewer opportunities to talk about gritter lorries.

Reason Five: You thought you'd sussed lift and toilet etiquette with your superiors through expertly practised wall-staring and urinary retention. Now, however, in the new classless canteen, you're faced with the prospect of introducing yourself or discovering for some more worrying reason your legendary reputation precedes you. Maybe have a sandwich at your desk. It's easier.

We didn't touch your half-eaten
Curry Snack Pot, honest.
Five reasons to hate …

Staff Meetings

Reason One: For the only time in their working lives all staff are equal – a malfunctioning microwave creates an existential void that no one can escape. But the staff meeting can only be acrimonious as no one ever feels 100 per cent happy at work, especially if a stand-up self-tanning centre has yet to be installed.

Reason Two: From filthy fridges to tea-bag thefts, it's the same yawn-inducing agenda every time, because nobody cares or ever does anything. But at least it's a revelation to senior staff, who are forced to descend from the heights of strategic decision making to the world of salmonella yoghurts.

Reason Three: New staff are encouraged to volunteer for the Christmas Party Committee, only to find themselves immediately faced with the Tudor-bethan 'let's roast an ox!' and Victorian 'I can't wait to wear a bonnet!' factions – and run out screaming.

Reason Four: Latent staff paranoia is rife as bosses are accused of sabotaging Secret Santa for corporate ends and getting staff ideas free from the suggestion box – ideas that consultants would charge thousands of pounds a day for, while wearing nice Prada suits too.

Reason Five: Staff surveys are discussed ad infinitum as people worry whether to reply: (a) 'No, I don't think I have a job for life but I don't think this is a reason to make me redundant.'; (b) 'Yes, I do think I have a job for life but this doesn't make me a slacker.'; (c) 'Beam me up, Scottie.'

Just know your place and
stay there, please.
Five reasons to hate …
Status

Reason One: We've all heard about the scaling down of middle management – but we all know who's given their jobs and silly titles and a bottom-of-range company car with an Xmas-tree-shaped deodoriser. And don't even think about working from home – you shirker.

Reason Two: Anyone with 'strategic' in their job title will never actually deliver anything, can't say what they do in words of one syllable, and has a strange relationship with their flip chart.

Reason Three: You know you're an important person in a meeting if: (a) you seriously have no idea where the refreshments come from; (b) you can't say hello without a PowerPoint presentation; (c) when you mention 'walking in the woods', everyone, apart from you, breathes a sigh of relief and makes for the door.

Reason Four: Corporate gifts, like bottles of vintage wine with antique dust and spa weekends with a chance to meet Gloria Hunniford, are meant to suggest you've arrived. Biros that don't work, calendars and pants with company logos mean you haven't even started.

Reason Five: No one can work out which is worse, status-wise: the open-plan office (your colleagues keep saying 'you don't have to be mad to work here but it helps' as if this is actually funny) or the sad, size-reduced office (your colleagues keep saying, 'we have a profit-driven culture of excellence', except it isn't meant to be funny). Hot-desking means 'I'm out of the office so much it doesn't matter' or 'where has my desk gone?'. You know who you are.

You seriously think you're
going places?
Five reasons to hate …
Summer Outings

Reason One: Reckoned to be a good thing as they allow senior management to offer staff, currently excited even by the idea of a fire drill, a trip to Legoland that clients refused as too embarrassing. They believe it can only increase motivation and, er, Lego-building skills.

Reason Two: In fact, outings are quite like the office Christmas party except with wasps – but without any mythical sex on photocopiers/in stationery cupboards/on boardroom tables. Pretty boring then.

Reason Three: Outing destinations say a lot about how valued you are: arriving at Wimbledon in a horse and carriage for strawberries and cream with Andre Agassi says 'we love you', while a barbecue in a local park with resident hoodies says 'if you complain, you won't get your free lolly'.

Reason Four: Your colleagues are just as tedious and socially inept outside the office – except it's more difficult to hide behind a tree and claim you were inundated with work. Try and forget the mustard for the sausage rolls – it'll give you something to talk about.

Reason Five: Nobody can quite get their head around how they're supposed to enjoy themselves, especially as your boss will want to take charge of your leisure time too and ask: (a) 'Now has anyone any interesting anecdotes about the luggage carousel at Heathrow?'; (b) 'Alright then, does anyone have any interesting anecdotes about anything at all?'; (c) 'Who'd like to do a company-mission-statement karaoke on the way back?' At least you'll have a fire drill to look forward to.

They have ways of making
you even more paranoid.
Five reasons to hate …
Surveillance

Reason One: 'You have called up an illegal website and will be reported to your Head of Department.' Who do they think they are, these Patronising Cyberspace Big Brothers of Supposed Taste and Decency? Sorry, you're not even sure what the current banned words are – though you'd be surprised if they don't include 'holidays', 'pleasant surroundings' and 'short meetings'.

Reason Two: The Italian Office Bic Biro Job; Lock, Stock and Barrel of Industrial Catering Coffee; The Talented Office Toilet Roll Thief Mr Ripley. They actually think we'd want to steal anything from their disgusting office? Yeah, right.

Reason Three: What's the difference between being a child and an office worker? Not a lot really, except the former doesn't get its phone calls recorded, have a swipe card monitoring its every movement or an appraisal that criticises its toilet visits. As for 'flexible working' at home, watch management get its knickers in a twist: honestly, can you really be trusted not to be moonlighting for the next Pop Idol?

Reason Four: They complain we send office emails to each other and to friends that aren't always about Transforming Cubicle Performance. Is it surprising, when they expect us to work 24/7, eat at our desks and see sticky melamine as a major theme in our lives? Makes *Nineteen Eighty-Four* seem like a minor case of rat infestation by comparison.

Reason Five: Please spare us those sad handwritten signs (or even sadder word-processed ones) from the Office Kitchen Neighbourhood Watch Committee. Under no circumstances known to humankind would we wish to touch their fetid bottle of milk, furry sandwiches or cracked Holly Hobby saucer, OK?

You probably need this like a
paintball through the head.
Five reasons to hate …

Team Building

Reason One: Jumping on each other in inflatable sumo wrestling suits, horse-whispering, white-water rafting, laughter therapy … it's puerile, it's juvenile, it's a load of testosterone-driven blokes arguing over who gets to blow up the horse's nostrils first, which means it might actually work as far as your colleagues are concerned.

Reason Two: Quite what paintballing has to do with team bonding apart from making a lot of poor trees look like something out of *a Charlie and the Chocolate Factory* film set and giving anyone in a secret military organisation an unfair advantage is quite beyond us.

Reason Three: Essential skills every team-building activity develops include sharing (usually one Kit Kat among twenty people); leadership (one person volunteers to contact the International Court of Human Rights); strategic thinking (going to the pub while two middle managers fight about who found the treasure); creativity (going to a shop and buying a raft); and lateral thinking (throwing a sickie).

Reason Four: We all know that under no circumstances should we ever: (a) beat our boss at constructing something unidentifiable from outsized Lego; (b) tell the Chief Executive he's blowing up the wrong part of the horse's anatomy; (c) laugh at the humour in the workplace consultant before he's actually said something.

Reason Five: The only time your team bonds is back in the office during the debrief session, when they tell HR that standing in the rain in a wood outside Luton wearing a tabard isn't corporate *joie de vivre* as we know it.

It's just a horrible rumour, don't worry.
Five reasons to hate ...

Teamwork

Reason One: To claim you're not a teamworker is like saying, 'I have the personality and vocabulary of a Dalek and the social skills of Attila the Hun.' Teamwork is reckoned to be the new sex and if you're not doing it, you're seriously folk music. Those who claim to be such brilliant teamworkers are usually the most selfish, aggressive and Machiavellian individuals going. They've got it sussed.

Reason Two: Saying you're a 'good teamplayer' is rather like claiming 'I talk to other people occasionally' or 'I enjoy breathing in company'. It's not you – it's them.

Reason Three: Inevitably, it requires 'team building', which we all know involves: (a) embarrassing bonding exercises in which you stand in circles and hug quiet colleagues; (b) a *Da Vinci* Treasure Hunt in the office to reduce everyone's mental age to eight, so that at least you all have something in common; (c) dangerous kayaking or mountaineering with at least one near-death experience, and everyone forced to ask some key questions – mainly what the hell are we doing here?

Reason Four: A team isn't a team if team leaders aren't busy learning new motivational skills (mainly, 'do this, or you're sacked'). Only don't complain – otherwise you'll be told you're not a teamplayer and forced to go on an arts-based training course, role-playing Henry V with you as a soldier. Guess who gets to die first …

Reason Five: It's recrimination hell at team meetings. But when it all goes wrong at least you have plenty of other people to blame – apart from yourself, of course. It smells like real team spirit to us.

If it's Tuesday, it must be, er, more filing. Five reasons to hate …
Temp, Being a

Reason One: Everyone enviously claims you're The Future – you with your excellent portfolio skills, frequent holidays and never needing to take office politics seriously. But at the same time they suggest you can't hold down a proper job. We just wish they'd make up their minds. After all, someone's got to be given the wobbly desk and the coffee cup with the indelible lipstick stain.

Reason Two: No one bothers to ask your name, which means they end up calling you: (a) by the previous temp's name; (b) Darlene, because they think all temps are Australian; (c) whistling and making strange sounds in the vague hope that the right vowel combination comes up; (d) nothing because after a week it's just too embarrassing.

Reason Three: You'll almost certainly be given the PC that belongs in an industrial museum with a printer that everyone claps when a sheet of paper comes out. You'll also of course be doing all the jobs no one else wants to do. Apart from filing, these include replying to the most aggressive customer complaints and making your single-handed contribution to the EEC Data Mountain.

Reason Four: Factions, in-groups, whingers, email flaming – office politics is the same everywhere. It's surprising offices actually do any work at all. Sorry, they don't – you do. The silver lining is that at least they let you get on with their work.

Reason Five: If you're a male temp, they decide you must be an actor who hasn't worked since *Family Affairs*, gay, or someone who isn't really trying. Everyone knows that to type, multi-task and make coffee successfully you must be a woman: please don't make things complicated.

And you thought having a favourite rubber was strange.
Five reasons to hate …

Things You Only Do in the Office

Reason One: You live inhumanely in a restricted MDF space performing a monotonous, repetitive task – if you were an animal there would be a televised appeal for your release. As it is, you're forced to express yourself in bizarre ways, such as stealing other people's chairs while they're away, collecting biscuits from meetings, and feeling violated if your litter bin is moved.

Reason Two: You display rows of unpleasant-looking, out-of-date medicines. These reveal to colleagues that you: (a) are seriously neurotic and this is a cry for help; (b) have an unpleasant infection that doesn't seem to be clearing up; (c) missed out on playing doctors and nurses when young and are now making up for lost time.

Reason Three: You have a strange sadistic relationship with a sad, mutant plant you inherited that defies the laws of science by staying alive – even though you fail to water it for weeks on end and pour your colleague's Moldavian Goat's Liver Tequila gift on it.

Reason Four: No matter how middle class you are and how often you shop in Marylebone High Street, in the office kitchen you'll soon find yourself stealing other people's milk, never washing up and using a cloth that resembles the Turin Shroud.

Reason Five: You find yourself discovering your child within by: (a) celebrating anything with helium balloons and an M&S sponge; (b) having a lifelong feud with a colleague because they touched your emergency anorak; (c) playing computer games which require the skills level of a two-year-old. Bless.

Sorry, break-out activity
doesn't mean running away.
Five reasons to hate ...
Training Courses

Reason One: You rarely know how useless they are until it's too late and you're inside a size-disadvantaged hotel room with a facilitator called Geoff or Pam and twenty other perspiring people, where everyone sits terrified in the back row for the 'Setting the Framework' session.

Reason Two: Don't forget the de rigueur warm-up exercise that likes to ask trainees which fruit or vegetable they most wish to identify with and why. Something British reserve has kept at bay for years is destroyed in seconds as Val from Welwyn Garden City reveals she has definite banana tendencies.

Reason Three: They always claim to make redundant the course you went on last time; not very difficult when it was called Developing Team Objectives: Part 5. You just know that within ten minutes your facilitator will have you making a beanstalk out of yesterday's newspaper. Trainers, incidentally, like to call themselves facilitators so they don't have to take responsibility for what's happening.

Reason Four: Brainstorming is just another word for flip-chart hell as you offer your random thoughts to the group on 'learning to say "no" in middle management'. Who would have thought 35 adults could spend two hours on 'Making the Most of Meetings' – and then decide the most important thing is to communicate?

Reason Five: Geoff and Pam claim to be responsive to every-one's learning style, which is why they do a PowerPoint presentation and then read it all out to the audience in case you, er, can't read. But think positive: at least the person with the 1982 Samsonite attaché case with 30 different Magic Markers wants to be your friend.

We're sorry you're feeling ill, but
it's no excuse, you know.
Five reasons to hate …

Unwell, Being

Reason One: No one believes you when you ring in to describe your illness. They're used to regular shirkers who can do a sickie with so much better Al Pacino method acting than you – it's those little lurid touches involving mucous membranes that count. Maybe best to be honest and say you've just got a little light sniffle.

Reason Two: How ill do you have to be before you can justify staying at home in today's 24/7 climate? The only answer is either looking like Mr Blobby – bloated and pink with yellow spots – or being dead.

Reason Three: Don't expect any sympathy from colleagues if you struggle in. Apart from your exciting new name (Typhoid Dave, Anthrax Annie) expect to become a social leper – especially if projectile vomiting is involved. Naturally your line manager is in a meeting all day so won't see you collapse. Do you do early evening performances as well as matinees?

Reason Four: Don't worry, the Office Wise Woman will have a holistic cure up her sleeve – usually something green that's been skimmed off the surface of a Third-World lake and is Liz Hurley's drug of choice. Alternatively, the First Aider – who's never had a real patient – can't wait to get a tourniquet round you and give you artificial respiration.

Reason Five: Remember, if you're working from home you're never ever allowed to be ill. Companies don't pay you to malinger in bedrooms with a list of so-called symptoms. Leave that to your office colleagues, please.

After you with the sick bucket,
Fluffy Bunny.
Five reasons to hate …
Valentine's Day

Reason One: Sixty per cent of us apparently find romance at work and many of us are living together and refusing to check out horse-and-carriage bridal packages. But we're still expected to dream of being Cuddles at the first shop sighting of burgundy padded velvet hearts and teddies in Valentine's bibs.

Reason Two: Basically, subtract twenty years from your real age and divide by the number of times you've ever entered Clinton Cards and you'll get an idea of the mental age expected of you.

Reason Three: If your idea of sexual liberation is having a set of 'Make me Late for Work' matching pillow cases then you'll be ready for Valentine's Day 'raunch' gifts – from a *Kama Sutra* puzzle to Love Doctor Prescription Kits. At least your colleagues will have someone to make sexually suggestive comments to – after all, it's nearly 300 days until the office Christmas party.

Reason Four: A bunch of specially delivered flowers makes everyone else feel unloved and depressed. A bunch of flowers delivered without an addressee only results in most of your office doing a distressing impersonation of Bridget Jones. And you thought the original was a bit psychopathic?

Reason Five: If you receive no Valentine's card or gift, it's automatically assumed that you're either a sad singleton or having a secret affair and thought you could keep it that way. It's why they'll make sure you try out the Executive Balls Scratcher during the marketing meeting. Don't be a spoil-sport …

Er, we're still waiting for that
iconic moment.
Five reasons to hate …
Water Cooler, The

Reason One: Expectations were unfairly raised about water-cooler conversations after hearing characters in *Ally McBeal* and *West Wing*. Except theirs were generally interesting, with impeccable timing, laugh lines and about 26 scriptwriters. Yours, on the other hand, are usually whinges about your workload and who designs those pointy paper cups you can't put down, and usually make you want to, er, scream.

Reason Two: In business, a 'turning point' is reckoned to be reached when something becomes a water-cooler moment. In which case, expect Alan Sugar to be green with envy as your colleagues' interesting conversation about gingernuts sweeps the country.

Reason Three: Thanks to open-plan offices, text messages, camera phones and emailing, we've already heard everything said at the water cooler before. Seriously, we've had the director's cut, DVD extras and podcast, and that 'love knobs' email sent by Emma to the MD by mistake is about as secret as Jordan's wedding.

Reason Four: Water coolers provide all the free team building that senior management pays thousands of pounds for to let you experience hypothermia and other colleagues' backsides on dangerous Welsh mountains.

Reason Five: They're always empty. The Woman Who Must Have Three Litres Of Water A Day and thinks she's a camel has just beaten the rest of you to it. Get ready, then, for the tapwater and the forty people it's already passed through conversation. Most refreshing.

And they're telling us to work
smarter. We're confused.
Five reasons to hate …
Workaholics

Reason One: These driven people like to set the benchmarks for the rest of us, which mainly consist of: (a) working until 11 pm and then apologising for going home; (b) not even having a presenteeism cardigan; (c) asking to be excluded from the EEC 48-hour work directive – and do they really have to stay at home on Christmas Day?

Reason Two: High-status workaholics like to impress us with their BlackBerries and claim, with martyred look, there's never a second when clients can't contact them. Lower-status workaholics dream about the 618 emails that will be waiting for them next morning and try not to get too excited.

Reason Three: They're the inspiration for, and the authors of, those essential management tomes our boss thinks we should read, from 'Seven Habits of Highly Effective People Who Haven't Read Their Children a Bedtime Story In Over a Decade' to 'Feel the Fear of Holidays and Have One Anyway'.

Reason Four: They like to make the rest of us feel guilty because we still hanker after a: (a) minimal lunch; (b) social life; (c) sex life. We're doing everything we can to keep them a secret, honest.

Reason Five: We try not to giggle when the workaholic organisation tells us to be even more 'focused' and 'work smarter' as it obviously hasn't done a lot for them. Look, if God had wanted us to hang around horrible office furniture late at night He would have given us a nicer range of Snack Pots.

This is real life. Don't laugh.
Five reasons to hate …

Work Experience

Reason One: You thought having essay crises and living off Curry Pot Noodles was depressing. But now your new (fortunately temporary) jealous colleagues are muttering 'welcome to the real world', reminding you about your student debt equivalent to the GNP of Haiti and suggesting you might like to work remotely, i.e. they're not giving you a chair or desk.

Reason Two: You're a kind of über-temp – given the work even your lowliest colleagues refuse. This includes: (a) sorting out fifteen years of filing; (b) speaking to nasty cold callers; (c) auditing rubber bands.

Reason Three: Judging by the general incompetence of your new colleagues, it seems that 'work experience' lasts a lifetime for most people. At least you can claim to be on a learning curve – the rest of your colleagues got lost somewhere in the middle and are still listed as missing. Don't worry, only another 40 years to go.

Reason Four: If you're very unlucky, you'll have to shadow one of their high-powered executives. This will involve attending endless meetings where everyone feels sorry for you because you don't know any acronyms and seem to think the English language can be used in the workplace. They'll soon put you right.

Reason Five: From 'experienced events manager' (had to organise own leaving party because no one else would) and 'strategic thinker' (successfully avoided doing any real work) to 'sings from the same corporate hymn sheet' (there was only one, I forgot to do the photocopying), only you know what those great work experience skills on your CV really mean.

How to know you're doing it all wrong – and feel like shit. Five reasons to hate …

Work Gurus

Reason One: If we didn't feel depressed, unsuccessful and unattractive, work gurus wouldn't make a living. They prey on our hopes, dreams and fears, suggesting we: (a) work harder; (b) work smarter; (c) learn some strategies from great historical figures like Sun Tzu (pretend to be wise), Machiavelli (pretend to agree with everyone), and Clausewitz (pretend to have a moustache).

Reason Two: *Who Moved My Stapler? ... The One-Minute Manager's Highly Effective Toilet Habits ... How to Win Friends and Influence People by Pretending to Actually Like the Bastards!* Derivative, repetitive and ridiculously upbeat, their titles can be summed up in a few words: don't work in an office if you can help it. It's all rather depressing and stressful – their publishers are banking on it.

Reason Three: Recessions and redundancies are just an opportunity for gurus to tell their readers about desperate self-employment opportunities, usually involving back bedrooms and then asking your boss if you can please come back. If all else fails they recommend a personal crystal (more accurate forecasts than the market at present) and self-hypnosis (tell yourself this isn't really happening).

Reason Four: They like to pretend to be 'one of us' and want to tell us how they solved their work/life balance problem – by getting out of the workplace at the earliest opportunity. Duh, if only we'd thought of that.

Reason Five: Whenever there's a new survey of workplace issues, they can be relied on for a concerned and lucrative press quote: 'Stress is a great problem. Something needs to be done about it.' Is that helpful or is that helpful?

You must be so happy with
no career structure.
Five reasons to hate …

Working from Home

Reason One: Working from home is hyped as the New Age working situation: environmentally friendly, stress-busting, etc. Actually, it just gives a new lease of life to can't-believe-their-luck Mormons and Betterware reps. But don't worry, there's always the local Small Businessman's Club if you want to bond with a dog shampooist and a burglar alarm salesman.

Reason Two: In a real office, everyone works with a common aim. At home, when you emerge grim-faced from your work-space, you find others grazing semi-comatose in front of *Murder She Wrote* asking you where the chocolate spread is. Suddenly ex-colleagues appear 'pleasantly eccentric' and overarching management just 'victims of the system'.

Reason Three: People in offices can always say they're in a meeting if they don't want to talk to you. But the poor home worker can only resort to: 'Sorry, I'm dealing with the cat's litter tray.' It just doesn't have the same cachet.

Reason Four: Christmas is a lonely time for the home-aloner – even the dreaded office party takes on a Pickwickian glamour. All you can do is display the card from the dog shampooist – and hope she doesn't want to touch base in the New Year.

Reason Five: It's exhausting, being the repository of ex-colleagues' hopes and dreams and keeping up the required level of perkiness. But don't be too depressed, many will soon have the chance to experience your exciting new lifestyle firsthand – at the next corporate downsizing.

Er, who was last to the holiday
wallplanner again?
Five reasons to hate ...

Working in the
Summer

Reason One: You're jealous of your boss who has a window to illegally open and breathe in traffic fumes – despite the wrath of the Air-Conditioning Police. At least his office temperature isn't geared towards high sauna without the option of terry towelling. In the office kingdom, the person with one half-operating air duct is king.

Reason Two: The self-employed are obviously sitting by the pool with a laptop and iPod, thinking Zen thoughts. Or else are on breezy balconies doing a little light portfolio working. And you just know that travel reps – thanks, Channel 5 programmers – at this very minute will be having experimental sex with their most attractive clients. You're green – or more likely jaundice yellow under the neon strip lights.

Reason Three: OK, no one wants to be a teacher, but everyone knows that for six whole weeks they can write hopeless novels just for the fun of it, live in a dressing-gown with Marmite stains, and worry about their lampshade colours (but only if they want to). You can tell we're desperate.

Reason Four: Sorry, if you're a politician, we're not going to hear a whimper out of you this summer – you'll be in Barbados, Cape Cod, Tuscany, the Dordogne, etc. It's a hard life making all those funny grunting sounds in the House of Commons.

Reason Five: Not forgetting colleagues who got to the holiday wallplanner first. But don't be bitter: at least you've got your two-day 'Christmas is for Cowards' break to look forward to (er, you hope).

Circle of Friends or *Scream 3*?
Only you know which.
Five reasons to hate …
Work Reunions

Reason One: Do you really want to see an ex-colleague who had: (a) Bon Jovi lyrics as an email sign-off; (b) an unnatural interest in how often you washed your gloves; (c) a disgusting box of used tissues on their desk for three years? And why are they looking for you? Be afraid – be very afraid.

Reason Two: Other methods of reviving your career having failed; you're desperately searching on 'Friends Reunited' for networking opportunities with that ex-colleague who apparently made it big. We don't like to worry you, but if they're such big hitters, why are they doing the same?

Reason Three: Please, how much do work colleagues really have in common apart from a mutual toleration of: (a) your boss; (b) other colleagues; (c) blank walls. Break this gently to the person who's desperate to organise 'The Toner Team: The Legendary Faxing Years 1993–97' Reunion.

Reason Four: Reminiscing down office memory lane – do you recall those golden times when you recycled your Secret Santa present from last year because you couldn't be bothered, or had to mirror a colleague's learning style (i.e. screamed back at them). We thought so. It sounds more like a self-help group for the terminally masochistic to us.

Reason Five: If you really have an obsessive desire to bring together a group of disparate and grudging people, you may be better off organising Christmas celebrations for your family. At least when everyone argues and it all turns out like a Mike Leigh script, no one's that surprised.

No, we love robins in waistcoats, really.
Five reasons to hate …
Xmas Cards, Office

Reason One: That pic of the Quality Street woman with a muff on the cards you sent to clients wasn't your choice, honest. Neither was the creepy corporate message ('Have a Prosperous New Year' – why don't they just say 'Continue Raping Half the Planet' and stop being coy?).

Reason Two: Get ready for the subliminal messages from your colleagues. If it's not an angelic host from Communications ('at least they're singing from the same hymn sheet'), it's your deadly rival's Christmas doves ('still pecking around for crumbs, loser?') and don't forget HR's Father Christmas ('here at least is someone who always meets his targets').

Reason Three: The boss doesn't have to send the same card to everyone – but we know he always does. Give him a break and let him go for that super bumper box of identical crap cards. He loves you all.

Reason Four: Look, we didn't think we were very special – but an electronic Xmas card of a flashing snowman that crashes our PC and is sent to 300 people isn't really very personal. Delete, delete.

Reason Five: What, no cards? Let's not forget those colleagues who see Scrooge as their Xmas role model. They must: (a) be too busy to remember that you like cuddly reindeer with anthropomorphic tendencies; (b) have given the money for your lovely card to charity; (c) seem to think you don't exist (and you thought it was just the temp). Make sure the Do They Know It's Christmas Karaoke With No Inhibitions Team visits their desks. First song: 'Sexual Healing'.

Resistance is useless – just put on the flashing reindeer antlers.
Five reasons to hate …
Xmas Countdown, The

Reason One: Just because you're a PA, doesn't mean you're obliged to buy emergency Xmas lingerie and a Paris weekend break for the boss's wife, or visit Toys Я Us for his offspring's presents. Personal Christmas Shopper isn't in the job description.

Reason Two: Half of your office is in a state of extreme anxiety with conversations asking why: (a) Nigella doesn't have a tip on how to make M&S mince pies look home-made; (b) Gary Rhodes ever had to go and glaze Brussels sprouts. Men just look sheepish and dodgy.

Reason Three: Those left in the office do their best to pretend they're not really standing around on stained carpet tiles but are having a Wonderful Christmas Experience. This generally revolves around eating the sixteenth packet of suppliers' chocolates, drinking gut-wrenching plonk and watching a one-minute version of *The Snowman* on someone's PC. Don't all rush.

Reason Four: As the Christmas cards arrive on your desk, each one tells a sad sender story: animals grubbing around for morsels in the cold (from non-managerial staff); Father Christmas with fat sack (from MD – he's keeping mum about his latest financial package); Old Masters' Nativity Scene (from multinational client – they own it). You, of course, gave your colleagues a non-descript snow scene (couldn't be bothered).

Reason Five: You've all been asked to join in a Secret Santa and purchase a gift for another staff member. You can hardly wait – though they turn out to include a Military Tattoo CD, a car ice-scraper, a packet of pasta, and half a salad spinner. Happy Christmas.

The corporate jargon, the boys' talk …
can we go home now?
Five reasons to hate …
Yes, We Have No Bananas

Reason One: Synergy – Bearing in mind our limited amounts of energy, it's now felt advisable to partner with another department or company with slightly less sloth-like qualities and then to declare that a Michelangelo moment has occurred with much electricity flowing between the finger of God and a previously lifeless Adam. Hopefully you are now more than the sum of your parts, although you won't expect to do any of the work.

Reason Two: Big Picture – Somewhere outside our cubicle is the scary real world, full of frightening customers, which none of us, quite rightly, wishes to come into contact with. But when your boss refers to the 'big picture' and a 'reality check', no one is sure if he means: (a) life, the universe and everything must now be included in your targets; (b) a supplier should be sent an Xmas card, otherwise you won't get a gear knob pen with cuff-links again next year.

Reason Three: Reinventing – We're supposed to be continually reinventing our product/company/selves. But we're also told not to reinvent the wheel because – as our boss says in his best 'can't do' voice – 'if it ain't broke, don't fix it'. We just wish they'd make up their minds.

Reason Four: Step Change – We're always being encouraged to make significant improvements in all aspects of our working lives. That's why we feel our boss's 'one giant step change for man, one small leap for mankind' claim was more than merited by our decision to become more grown up and dress our Beanie Babies in corporate mission-wear. We hope it makes him happy.

Reason Five: Rocket Science – When people say 'it's not rocket science' in meetings, they usually mean: 'I haven't really got a clue what I'm talking about but I'm still going to bore you for twenty minutes.' Some of us dream of working at Cape Canaveral just to scream 'YES!' when they say 'it's rocket science'.

We're very tired – please
do not disturb.
Five reasons to hate ...

Zzzzzzzz

Reason One: If rudely woken up, provided you make one vaguely comprehensible comment during the finance meeting they should leave you alone. It can be 'where am I?', 'who are you?', or 'you sound like an alien invader: please take me straight to your spacecraft'. What do they expect when you got home at 2 pm last night and your partner failed to recognise you?

Reason Two: Falling asleep during a brainstorming session is more acceptable as: (a) most people are so embarrassed anyway and may not notice you snoring; (b) they might think it's your 'learning style'; (c) they won't mind you saying something stupid when you wake up – after all, everyone else already has.

Reason Three: 'Power-napping' … 'the final stage of my 'Neuro-Linguistic Programming' course' … 'I'm really awake' … you're fed up with always having to justify your occasional resort to some emergency shut-eye at your desk because of the pressures of corporate life. Next time you'll just go to a meeting and get your proper entitlement like everyone else, OK?

Reason Four: Admittedly you can always fall asleep in the staff room but you're worried that you may become a passive inhaler of industrial strength portions of J-Lo and never regain consciousness.

Reason Five: Finding another passenger falling asleep on your shoulder on a commuter train isn't a very edifying experience. In fact it's probably a wake-up call for both of you – especially if the other person is in the first stages of REM and is currently dribbling long spools of spittle down your new suit. Just think of it as the first day of the rest of your commuting life …

The Corporate
Bullshit Detector

*The A–Z of jarring jargon – for everyone
who's been there and wishes they hadn't*

A

Action planning – To avoid doing it on the back of an envelope at the last minute, you spend weeks defining your goals, assigning tasks and reviewing schedules. Then real life happens, not to mention other people's action plans, and you end up doing it on the back of an envelope at the last minute.

Added value – Producing a product or service, then realising you need to find extra uses to make it sound more attractive. Results range from touting Häagen-Dazs as a sex aid to claiming your company is a professional organisation.

Aims – Does anyone really know the difference between business aims and objectives apart from Sue your trainer, and does it really matter? If she knows so much, why is her company still based on an industrial estate on the outskirts of Milton Keynes?

B

Balancing home and work – There's bound to be one smug woman in your office who claims not to have a recently thawed spinach lasagne or a pair of wet children's pants in their bag. Where are they from – Planet Madonna?

Benchmark – If your brilliant, new state-of-the-art product can't be benchmarked or compared with what somebody did last year in Basingstoke, you might as well forget it.

C

Competencies – Out go those long job histories and lists of hobbies. In come those traits and behaviours that prove our capabilities and even suggest we're vaguely competent. Apparently.

Core worker – Somebody they can't sack because they saw what the MD was doing on the photocopier at the last Christmas party.

D

Damage limitation – Shooting yourself in the foot – as opposed to other parts of your anatomy.

Downtime – They even manage to make having your Hobnob sound impressive.

E

Emotional leakage – Used to be called crying.

Empowered – Everybody claims to be empowering everyone else – mainly by letting them take on so many extra responsibilities they don't have time to notice their salary hasn't gone up. The only truly empowered person around is the MD's wife: she's got a Harrods account card and doesn't have to work.

Event horizon – Hijacking of a scientific term for a mega-concept like you've never seen. Break it to your MD gently that this probably doesn't describe your company's annual report.

Exit strategy – Dreaming up a series of unpleasant mystery illnesses and dental appointments in preparation for your secret interviews and, please God, leaving party.

F

Facilitator – If you're on a training course called 'Find Your Inner Child in Spreadsheet Management', your trainer will like to call themselves a facilitator. This way they won't have to take any personal responsibility for the gibberish and boredom you face over the next eight hours.

Fast-tracker – Someone who won't stay long enough to know where the emergency tea bags are kept.

Focused – Person who likes to boast that they're able to concentrate on one thing at a time. A bit sad when you come to think about it.

G

Game plan – Everybody is supposed to have one for the next five years with built-in career reviews and life-training. Or else just needs to remember to buy more lottery tickets.

Gap in the market – Sinclair C5 car, Tom Jones doing hip-hop, retro pussy-bow blouses. Tell your boss that some gaps in the market are meant to be.

Grass roots – The depressing people who buy your products or services. Every head office insists it's in touch with theirs, and someone once remembers running a focus group in Chelmsford.

Group culture – Sharing the same aims and objectives – chiefly going home occasionally if at all possible.

H

Homeworking – Very holistic, but have you lost your work status and pension plan just to be on first-name terms with the local Betterware representative?

Hot desking – Used by those who are too important to be in the office very often – or so unimportant that it doesn't really matter. You know who you are.

I

Increments – The minimalist office seems to have encouraged minimalist salary increases. Ask for a magnifying glass so that you can see yours more clearly.

In the loop – Those who use the same impenetrable jargon, and see themselves as cutting-edge and belonging to a secret society of true believers. More like round the bend.

Investors in people – Lots of silver plaques explaining that your employer is as caring as it can get without actually treating you to an Aveda body spa or paying you more.

ISO 9000 – If you are not involved with this benchmarking system, you'll have no idea what it is. Even if you are, you'll probably have the same problem.

J

Japanese-style management – The collapse of the Japanese economy has rather put the mockers on this one. If you've still got a Japanese management system in your company, start considering hari-kari.

Job-depth – Check the size of your job description. If it only runs to a single page, then think 'flexible work force'.

Job share – Both of you should be eternally grateful that your company is willing to let you do what is virtually a full-time job each for just half the pay.

Job-specific competencies – Surprisingly, some jobs require you to actually know something – don't worry, in your case Outlook Express (social calendar mapped out for the next five years) or art therapy (exchanging doodles during a meeting) will be quite sufficient.

Joint implementation – Both partners agree to actually do the same thing together at the same time. Don't they make it look like hard work? Sometimes you wonder if you've missed something.

Just in time – Supply-on-demand system for maximum efficiency, which includes periods of inactivity; sort of what you are expected to do all of the time, except without the periods of inactivity.

K

Key – Players, objectives, actions, visions, outcomes. What is it about this adjective that makes everything very important, self-important or just plain ridiculous? Urgent key guidance needed immediately please.

Knowledge economy – Fewer and fewer of us are making widgets and, instead, are supposed to be exhaustively producing ideas and concepts in the form of symbolic knowledge. Just in case we ever wanted an excuse for an emergency lie-down.

Know where all the bodies are buried – Oh, dear, should you report this?

L

Leadership skills – Better write yours down for the boss – you won't be around forever.

Leading-edge – Your company is probably leading-edge in the same way that London Underground is a transport system or Victoria Beckham is a singer. Best not to inquire too much, really.

Leave it up to the man on the coalface – Probably a woman, but a mere detail.

Let's put that in the lift and see which floor it stops at – Yours.

Life-cycle assessment – Is there any real reason for your company and its systems, products or services to exist? Don't answer that.

Low-hanging fruit – Easy pickings for your company that even it might get right for once.

M

Macro-management – The big stuff – don't expect to know anything about this. No one else does.

Managing change – Has obviously struck a chord, as every job description requires it. Though a little like asking a fish how it deals with water.

Meet the needs – Of your customers, your company, your boss, your plant. Everyone seems to have needs as far as you can see, apart from you.

Mentor – Someone whose job you would like to have who sits and listens to you and suggests ten easy steps to get it.

Messenger – Whenever your boss has to impart bad news, he says he's only the messenger. If he insists on pretending he's from Parcelforce, tell him return to sender.

N

Nano – First of all they wanted everything in a nanosecond; now they would like it a bit quicker still.

Negative dialogues – What, you and your boss? See it more as keeping the channels of communication open – by several millimetres if you're lucky.

New customer acquisition strategy – So many meetings, consultancies, financial partners. Wouldn't it be cheaper just to give the product away?

New media channels – Your boss keeps fiddling with his Palm Pilot and sees himself as the next Bill Gates.

No-brainer – Alright, they were very obvious ideas, but they didn't have to be rude about them at the brainstorm session. In future you'll just doodle on your sugar paper, like everyone else.

Non-verbal communication – In an interview, what we say apparently means less than using the same body language as our interviewer. If we can find out what they'll be wearing in advance, we can go for full lookalike. After all, they're hardly going to refuse their long-lost sibling a job, are they?

O

Objectives – Sorry, *Cosmo*, this is the new Big O. If you're not hitting the peaks of performance, you can always fake it.

Obsession with the customer – Always number one with us, even when they scream down the phone and say they want to talk to a real person. We love it.

One-stop shop – You wish your boss wouldn't say this to your customers. It makes you feel like an all-night garage on Kilburn High Road with a nifty line in blue-dyed flowers and Dolly Parton karaoke tapes.

Ongoing process – You're dealing with one thing right, then up pops another one. Don't worry – once that's finished, expect an ongoing situation. Excuse us while we have an ongoing nervous breakdown.

Organisational excellence – It's nice of us to say it about ourselves, don't you think?

Outcomes – What the public sector has instead of profits, except that people see even less of them.

P

Pan-European – Your company has clients only in Gibraltar and Latvia – but this makes it sound much better.

Paradigm shift – Every company is supposed to have one of these; usually means they're trying to get you to the hot desk with three weeks of dirty cups.

People management – Well, usually.

Pitch – This is what we should be doing every minute of the day with colleagues and prospective employers, apparently. That's pitch yourself, not pinch yourself.

Portfolio of skills – Basically, makes all those unsuccessful career starts sound sexy on your CV.

Position statement – What you send out even before the mission statement has been written. Yes, that incomprehensible.

Process improvement teams – At college, no one ever told you about work areas like this. Or at the interview. Now you know why.

Process management – Everything's stripped down to its constituent parts and made easy. Like you working through the computer manual for your boss.

Procurement – Nothing at all to do with the attractive girl from Accounts who wears the very obvious Agent Provocateur bra.

Project management – Leading on the resource management interface always sounds like a killer on your CV, even if it's just clearing out your cupboard.

Public-private partnership – Market forces, outcomes, shareholders, stakeholders – all together in one room. We know.

Push the envelope – As far away from you as possible, especially if according to the job description you were doing only executive duties with a little light report writing.

Putting rocks on the runway – That's not very sensible, is it?

Q

Quality – Indefinable. Ineluctable. Holy Grail. Golden Fleece. Exactly. So how do they expect us to achieve it?

Quality Circle – They might not want you in the Groucho Club, but here's one group that'll welcome you with open arms. You can fall asleep with your colleagues discussing Quality Customer Service.

Quality Gate – Sort of like the Pearly Gate – you'll know it when you see it.

Quality Time – The time you spend outside your job, worrying about it.

R

Radar – We thought we had an in-built one for when the boss makes one of his rare appearances outside his glass-fronted office. We just wish we hadn't been looking at that story about the sex-mad DJ and the tortoise, and the screen hadn't frozen.

Raise a flag – We surrender – we'll reveal the secrets of the Implementation Management Team without a struggle. Take us to your leader.

Reality check – Sorry, tell your boss this isn't you and him sitting behind a mirror watching rather strange people in a focus group sharing their hopes, fears and dreams about your rather under-whelming product.

Refactoring – Sounds pretty nasty. Sure we'll end up having it done to us, whatever it is.

Remit – Haven't you had enough of hearing about everyone else's? What about yours for a change? Start with: 'I will only visit Starbucks for annoyingly complicated orders once a day.'

Revectored – It's annoying, isn't it, how often you have to have this redone – like Botox, we suppose.

Right size – Right size, downsize, smart size – can't they make their minds up?

R-plus – This can only be a classification for terrifying corporate videos denuded of unattractive employees and with Richard Clayderman soundtracks. That will be 'R' for retching, then?

Run it up the flagpole and see who salutes it – Only if carried by a pole-dancer, knowing your department.

S

Scuba in your think-tank – The team were quite resistant to wearing funny hats for that Edward de Bono brainstorming session. How are they going to react to swimming cozzies?

Self-marketing – A bit like self-help; no one else is going to do it for you, so you might as well do it for yourself.

Shareholder value – Caring way of saying 'maximum profits, please' without sounding too sordid.

Shelf life – Don't start getting worried, dear, you're the Sunny Delight of office life. You'll last forever.

Special projects – They can't decide what to do with you and your boss. This could be the start of something big (or small). Check the size of your flip chart and see how many pens they've given you.

Stakeholder – What public services have instead of shareholders. If you stand at a bus stop in the rain that makes you a stakeholder. Unfortunately, not quite as sexy as a big dividend cheque.

Steer better – Ask the cap'n of our ship about this, although we expect to be coming up from behind in a dinghy as usual, feeling queasy.

Stress management – From being told to drink more herbal tea to spending two weeks in The Priory – you'll soon learn how important or otherwise you are.

Superclusters – We can't help it if Carole Thatcher's public urination drew record crowds to the water cooler.

Sweating your assets – We thought that's what our air-conditioning system was doing already.

T

Tactics – The tedious bits of a strategy that actually help you to deliver it – in your case, the flame throwers you require as part of your 'Total Transformation of the Office Kitchen' strategy.

Teamwork – Consider how hard you all worked together to produce your 'We Love You, Robbie' office wall collage out of miniature Flumps. Now see if you can transfer that to something to do with work.

Thought leadership – Blimey, is that what the Chief Executive's speech was meant to be about: no wonder we didn't understand it.

Throughput – You wish the MD wouldn't say 'Thank you for your throughput, people' when he sees you once a year. Makes you feel like the cold tap. Or a large intestine.

Total Resources Unit – We're happier to say we're in marketing, if it's OK with you.

Touch base – Forcing yourself on to someone who in normal circumstances wouldn't wish to see you, but now doesn't have much choice. Marginally better than saying: 'Tell me something to my career advantage and don't just talk about nothing. What do you think this is, an episode of *Seinfeld*?'

U

User-friendly – Everything technological your company uses, until it breaks down and the person from IT tells you it will take two weeks and here's a Biro.

USP – We're all being told to list our unique selling points and make our CVs different from everyone else's. But maybe that shot of you kissing Wittgenstein's grave is making you out to be just a little too unique.

Utilisation – Tell the boss to stop saying this if he wants positive feedback for his 360-degree appraisal – he's not being filmed for the corporate video now.

V

Vertical ladders – So there is a way out, after all. After you, but don't look down.

Viral PR – Press officers producing press releases which no one reads, now complement these with web messages which no one reads either.

Virtual organisations – If we don't answer the phone very much and people don't think we're here, does that make our company one of these?

W

Window of opportunity – So embarrassing. When your three-year-old niece has a Burberry handbag and mobile phone and says she will try to find you a window, you know the zeitgeist has probably moved on.

Win-win scenario – It's good, we suppose, that the boss is so focused on success, but does he really have to compete for the frothiest cappuccino in the team every time?

Working in partnership – Someone who wants something from you and is prepared to endure your personality defects for a minimal period in order to get it, provided they can steal your best ideas and you do all the work.

Work through others – The boss knows we are mighty suspicious of the 'delegation' word. He could try this one, though; it may take us some time to work out that it means the same thing.

X

X Theory – The belief that most employees are lazy and lacking in ambition, and luncheon vouchers wouldn't improve them.

...heory – The belief that maybe luncheon vouchers might do ...e trick.

Z

Zero-sum negotiations – All very well when the boss wants maximum gains at a rival's expense – but a bit much when it's your salary increase. Who does he think he is, Tony Soprano?